THE TOTTENHAM HOTSPUR QUIZ BOOK

600 FUN QUESTIONS FOR SPURS FANS EVERYWHERE

JAMES CONRAD

Published by Blue Yonder Books

Introduction

The great fallacy is that the game is first and last about winning. It is nothing of the kind. The game is about glory, it is about doing things in style and with a flourish, about going out and beating the lot, not waiting for them to die of boredom.

Danny Blanchflower

This book has six hundred questions for all Tottenham supporters. The questions are about its history, its achievements, its players, its managers, and many other things that are to do with Spurs.

The questions are generally in a multiple-choice format and are of varying degrees of difficulty to test and increase the knowledge of all fans.

The Tottenham Hotspur Quiz Book is both entertaining and informative and will provide hours of memory wracking entertainment for Spurs fans.

Table of Contents

Quiz 1: The Start

1. **What year was Tottenham Hotspur founded?**

   a) 1878 b) 1882 c) 1886

2. **What was the first name of the club?**

   a) Hotspur Football Club b) Spurs Football Club c) Tottenham Football Club

3. **Spurs won the FA Cup in 1901. What record did they set which still stands?**

   a) The highest score in a final b) The largest crowd to watch a final c) The only non-league team to win the FA Cup

4. **Which year were they elected to the Football League?**

   a) 1892 b) 1900 c) 1908

5. **In 1898 who became the first manager of Spurs?**

   a) John Cameron b) Frank Brettell c) Fred Kirkham

6. **He resigned to following year to join Portsmouth. Why did he leave Spurs?**

   a) He was sacked b) His full time job moved out to Portsmouth c) Portsmouth offered substantially more money

7. **In the 1908 – 09 season they gained promotion from the Second Division to the first by finishing second to which team?**

   a) Bolton b) Hull c) West Brom

8. **On the 23rd April 1921 Spurs won their second FA Cup. Who did they beat?**

   a) Liverpool b) Man Utd c) Wolves

9. **How many years was it before they won the FA Cup again?**

   a) 20 years b) 30 years c) 40 years

10. **Who was the club's leading scorer on 5 occasions between 1908 – 9 and 1912 - 13?**

    a) Billy Minter b) Bert Bliss c) Jimmy Pass

Quiz 2: Bill Nicholson

1. **Where was Bill Nicholson born?**

   a) Scarborough b) Norwich c) Newcastle

2. **He played his first professional games for a club which was officially a Spurs 'nursery club'. Which club was this?**

   a) Margate b) Romford c) Northfleet

3. **In 1939 he joined who on the outbreak of war?**

   a) Royal Artillery b) Kings Own Yorkshire Light Infantry c) Durham Light Infantry

4. **How many league appearances did Nicholson make for Spurs?**

   a) 314 b) 422 c) 563

5. **How many trophies did he win as a player for Spurs?**

   a) 1 b) 2 c) 3

6. **What year was Nicholson appointed the manager of Spurs?**

   a) 1957 b) 1958 c) 1959

7. **How many times did Nicholson play for England?**

   a) 1 b) 15 c) 25

8. **Nicholson's first game as manager was against Everton at White Hart Lane. Spurs won but what was the score?**

   a) 4 – 3 b) 5 – 3 c) 10 - 4

9. **Nicholson resigned as manager of Spurs in September 1974. Which club did he become an adviser for?**

   a) West Ham b) Chelsea c) Arsenal

10. **How many trophies did he win as manager of Spurs?**

   a) 7 b) 9 c) 11

Quiz 3: Jimmy Greaves

1. **What is Greaves' middle name?**

   a) Phillip b) Peter c) Paul

2. **He began his professional career at which club?**

   a) Chelsea b) Tottenham c) West Ham

3. **He scored on his debut against which club?**

   a) Arsenal b) Tottenham c) Man Utd

4. **In June 1961 he was sold to which club?**

   a) AC Milan b) Juventus c) Roma

5. **Greaves was bought by Tottenham in December 1961. What was the fee?**

   a) £98,000 b) £99,999 c) £100,000

6. **Greaves played 320 league games for Tottenham. How many goals did he score?**

   a) 186 b) 209 c) 220

7. **In March 1970 Greaves left Spurs for West Ham. Who was he part exchanged for as part of the deal?**

   a) Martin Peters b) Billy Bonds c) Harry Redknapp

8. **Greaves played 57 times for England. How many goals did he score in those games?**

   a) 26 b) 38 c) 44

9. **In the 1966 World Cup he played in the first three games but was injured and replaced in the quarter finals and didn't regain his place in the tournament. Who replaced him?**

   a) Martin Peters b) Geoff Hurst c) Alan Ball

10. **From October 1985 to April 1992 Greaves presented a popular Saturday lunchtime program with which former footballer?**

    a) Ian St John b) Denis Law c) Ron Atkinson

Quiz 4: Jose Mourinho

1. **Which country was Mourinho born in?**

   a) Spain b) Italy c) Portugal

2. **In 2000 Mourinho took the job at Sporting CP as interpreter/coach to which manager?**

   a) George Graham b) Bobby Robson c) Graham Taylor

3. **What was the first team he managed?**

   a) Porto b) Benfica c) Inter Milan

4. **Who did Mourinho take over from as manager of Man Utd?**

   a) Van Gaal b) Giggs c) Moyes

5. **How many trophies did he win with Man Utd?**

   a) 1 b) 2 c) 3

6. **Mourinho has won the Champions League twice with which teams?**

   a) Real Madrid and Porto b) Inter Milan and Real Madrid c) Inter Milan and Porto

7. **On the 20th November 2019 Mourinho was appointed the manager of Tottenham. What was their league position when he took control?**

   a) 6th b) 10th c) 14th

8. **What position did they finish in the league in his first season in 2019 - 20?**

   a) 6th b) 10th c) 14th

9. **Who did Mourinho say helped Tottenham win 4 – 2 against Olympiacos in the Champions League in November 2019?**

   a) Referee b) Linesman c) Ball boy

10. **What did Mourinho call Arsene Wenger in 2005?**

    a) Worzel Gummidge b) A voyeur c) A spy

Quiz 5: Harry Redknapp

1. **What is Harry Redknapp's middle name?**

   a) Henry b) James c) Peter

2. **Which club's youth ranks did he play for between the ages of 11 – 15?**

   a) Tottenham b) West Ham c) Bournemouth

3. **In October 2008 who did Redknapp replace as manager of Tottenham?**

   a) Martin Jol b) Jacques Santini c) Juande Ramos

4. **What position in the Premier League were Spurs when Redknapp took over?**

   a) 20th b) 18th c) 16th

5. **What position did Spurs finish in Redknapp's first year in charge in 2008 – 09?**

   a) 5th b) 8th c) 11th

6. **Which national team has Redknapp managed?**

   a) Lebanon b) Jordan c) Egypt

7. **Who is Redknapp's nephew?**

   a) Frank Lampard b) Billy Bonds c) Steve Perryman

8. **In his 2007 trial for fraud Redknapp claimed to have problems reading and understanding contracts. This has not prevented him writing how many autobiographies?**

   a) 2 b) 3 c) 4

9. **How many trophies did Redknapp win as manager of Tottenham?**

   a) 0 b) 1 c) 2

10. **Which TV reality show was Redknapp in during 2018?**

    a) Strictly Come Dancing b) Dancing on Ice c) I'm a Celebrity

Quiz 6: Glenn Hoddle

1. **What year was Hoddle born?**

   a) 1955 b) 1956 c) 1957

2. **Who recommended a young Hoddle to Spurs?**

   a) Alan Gilzean b) Martin Chivers c) Jimmy Greaves

3. **Hoddle made his debut for Spurs on the 30th August 1975. Who was the manager that selected him?**

   a) Bill Nicholson b) Terry Neil c) Keith Burkinshaw

4. **This debut was against Norwich and he came on as a substitute. Who was he substituting?**

   a) Steve Perryman b) Joe Kinnear c) Cyril Knowles

5. **How many games did Hoddle play for Spurs?**

   a) 470 b) 490 c) 510

6. **How many England appearances did he make?**

   a) 53 b) 63 c) 73

7. **In 1987 Hoddle left Spurs to join which club?**

   a) Marseille b) PSG c) AS Monaco

8. **In March 2001 Hoddle was appointed the manager of Tottenham following the sacking of which manager?**

   a) Christian Gross b) George Graham c) Jacques Santini

9. **Hoddle suffered a cardiac arrest at the BT Sports studios, and it was only the quick actions of an employee, Simon Daniels, which saved his life. It was also Hoddle's birthday. How old was he?**

   a) 57 years old b) 59 years old c) 61 years old

10. **In 1987 Hoddle made a record called "Diamond Lights" and it peaked at number 12 in the charts. It was described as "...truly awful Dad dancing and shocking lyrics". Who co-starred with Hoddle in the singing of this song?**

    a) Paul Gascoigne b) Chris Waddle c) Gary Lineker

Quiz 7: Steve Perryman

1. **What is Perryman's middle name?**

   a) John b) Peter c) Paul

2. **Perryman played in the Spurs team that won the 1970 Youth Cup. Who was his midfield partner?**

   a) Graeme Souness b) Sammy Lee c) Terry McDermott

3. **How many years was Perryman at Spurs?**

   a) 15 b) 16 c) 17

4. **How many appearances did he make for Spurs?**

   a) 754 b) 854 c) 954

5. **He was the Football Writers Association 'Footballer of the Year' in which year?**

   a) 1982 b) 1984 c) 1986

6. **How many trophies did he win while at Tottenham?**

   a) 6 b) 8 c) 10

7. **In 1986 Perryman left Spurs and joined which club?**

   a) Watford b) Reading c) Oxford

8. **How many caps did Perryman get for England?**

   a) 0 b) 1 c) 2

9. **In July 1993 Perryman was appointed as the Assistant to which Spurs manager?**

   a) Ossie Ardiles b) Terry Venables c) Gerry Francis

10. **In 1990 Perryman took his first managerial role when he became the player manager at which club?**

    a) Watford b) Brentford c) West Ham

Quiz 8: Paul Gascoigne

1. **Where was Gascoigne born?**

   a) Newcastle b) Gateshead c) Sunderland

2. **Gascoigne made his debut for Newcastle on the 13th April 1985. Who was the Newcastle manager at the time?**

   a) Arthur Cox b) Jim Smith c) Jack Charlton

3. **At 18 Gascoigne signed a two year contract with Newcastle. How much was he paid?**

   a) £120/week b) £1200/week c) £12,000/week

4. **Before Gascoigne signed for Spurs which team had he agreed to join?**

   a) Man Utd b) Arsenal c) Leeds

5. **When Gascoigne signed for Spurs, he was given a £100,000 signing on fee. What did he spend £70,000 of this on?**

   a) A Lamborghini b) A casino c) A house for his parents

6. **What year was he named the BBC Sports Personality of the year?**

   a) 1990 b) 1991 c) 1992

7. **Gascoigne ruptured his cruciate ligament 15 minutes into the !991 FA Cup final with a reckless challenge. Who were the opponents?**

   a) Notts Forest b) Sheffield Weds c) Everton

8. **Who did Spurs sell Gascoigne to?**

   a) Roma b) Sampdoria c) Lazio

9. **How many league games did Gascoigne play for Spurs?**

   a) 92 b) 192 c) 292

10. **In 1990, following the World Cup, Gascoigne reached number 2 in the UK top 40 with a recording of what song?**

    a) World in motion b) World at your feet c) Fog on the Tyne

Quiz 9: Mauricio Pochettino

1. **Which country was Pochettino born in?**

   a) Uruguay b) Argentina c) Chile

2. **His first professional team was Newell's Old Boys based in Santa Fe. Who was the manager who gave him his debut?**

   a) Cesar Menotti b) Osvaldo Ardiles c) Marcelo Bielsa

3. **Which was the first European club he played for?**

   a) Real Madrid b) Espanyol c) Seville

4. **On the 27th May 2014 Pochettino became the Spurs manager. Who did he replace?**

   a) Tim Sherwood b) Andre Villas-Boas c) Harry Redknapp

5. **In his first season at Spurs, he took then to the final of the League Cup only to be beaten by which club?**

   a) Man City b) Chelsea c) Liverpool

6. **Spurs reached the 2019 Champions League Final under Pochettino with a fantastic comeback against which team in the semi-finals?**

   a) Barcelona b) Ajax c) Real Madrid

7. **How many games was he manager of Spurs?**

   a) 243 b) 293 c) 343

8. **On the 2nd May 2016 Spurs drew 2-2 with Chelsea. Which Premier League record did Spurs break that day?**

   a) Longest run of drawn games b) The longest run of unbeaten away games c) Most yellow cards by a team in a game

9. **In the 2016 -17 season Spurs finished 2nd in the Premier League to which team?**

   a) Chelsea b) Man City c) Leicester

10. **How many trophies did Pochettino win as manager of Spurs?**

    a) 0 b) 1 c) 2

Quiz 10: Terry Venables

1. **What is Venable's middle name?**

   a) Frederick b) Bartholomew c) Humphrey

2. **What was Venables first professional club as a player?**

   a) West Ham b) Crystal Palace c) Chelsea

3. **He was sold on to Spurs after he had fallen out with which manager?**

   a) Dave Sexton b) Tommy Docherty c) Malcolm Allison

4. **How many appearances did he make for Tottenham as a player?**

   a) 141 b) 181 c) 221

5. **How many games did Venables play for England?**

   a) 0 b) 2 c) 10

6. **What was his first managerial position?**

   a) Queens Park Rangers b) Middlesbrough c) Crystal Palace

7. **In 1984 he became manager of which Spanish club?**

   a) Real Madrid b) Barcelona c) Valencia

8. **In 1994 Venables became the England manager. Who did he take over from?**

   a) Graham Taylor b) Glenn Hoddle c) Bobby Robson

9. **Which other national team has Venables managed?**

   a) Qatar b) United Arab Emirates c) Australia

10. **Venables is also credited with being the co-creator of a TV detective series. What was it called?**

    a) Cracker b) Rebus c) Hazel

Quiz 11: Harry Kane

1. **What is Harry Kane's middle name?**

   a) Edward b) Andrew c) Charles

2. **Whose youth academy did he play for to begin with?**

   a) Chelsea b) Wolves c) Arsenal

3. **During his early career at Spurs, he was loaned out to several clubs. Which one was he not loaned to?**

   a) Leicester b) Norwich c) Crystal Palace

4. **On the 7th April 2014 Kane played his first Premier League game for Spurs. Who were the opposition?**

   a) Sunderland b) Newcastle c) Hull

5. **Which country, other than England, was Kane eligible to play for?**

   a) Wales b) Republic of Ireland c) Australia

6. **Kane has scored more than 25 goals in a Premier League season several times. Who was the previous Spurs player to get 25 goals in a season?**

   a) Berbatov b) Bale c) Lineker

7. **Kane attended Chingford Foundation School. Who had also attended this school?**

   a) Jimmy Greaves b) David Beckham c) Glenn Hoddle

8. **What year was Kane the PFA Young Player of the Year?**

   a) 2012/13 b) 2013/14 c) 2014/15

9. **Kane became the third quickest to score 100 league goals for Spurs in 138 games. Who was the quickest?**

   a) Jimmy Greaves b) Bobby Smith c) George Hunt

10. **What is Kane's dog called?**

    a) Gazza b) Brady c) Boris

Quiz 12: Gary Mabbutt

1. **What year was Gary Mabbutt born in?**

   a) 1959 b) 1961 c) 1963

2. **What was his first professional club?**

   a) West Brom b) Wolves c) Bristol Rovers

3. **Which manager signed Mabbutt for Spurs?**

   a) Terry Neil b) Peter Shreeves c) Jack Burkinshaw

4. **Which club claims that Mabbutt's knee won them the FA Cup?**

   a) Coventry b) Southampton c) Wimbledon

5. **What condition does Mabbutt suffer from?**

   a) Diabetes b) Asthma c) Agoraphobia

6. **In November 1993 Mabbutt suffered an horrific injury of a fractured skull and eye socket. Whose challenge caused the injury?**

   a) Vinnie Jones b) Alan Shearer c) John Fashanu

7. **How many appearances did Gary Mabbutt make for Spurs?**

   a) 511 b) 611 c) 711

8. **How many goals did he score in those games?**

   a) 38 b) 48 c) 58

9. **Which team did he support as a youngster?**

   a) Arsenal b) Chelsea c) West Ham

10. **How many trophies did he win while at Tottenham?**

   a) 1 b) 2 c) 3

Quiz 13: Pat Jennings

1. **What country was Jennings born in?**

   a) Wales b) Northern Ireland c) Republic of Ireland

2. Spurs signed Jennings in June 1964 from which club?

a) Brentford b) Leyton Orient c) Watford

3. How many games did he play for Spurs?

a) 496 b) 596 c) 696

4. In the 1967 Charity Shield Jennings scored a remarkable goal from his own penalty area. Who was the goalkeeper he beat at the opposite end?

a) Alex Stepney b) Tommy Lawrence c) Gordon Banks

5. In 1975 – 76 Jennings was the first goalkeeper to win the PFA Players Player of the Year Award. There have only been two to win this. Who was the other?

a) Peter Schmeichel b) Petr Cech c) Peter Shilton

6. In August 1977 Spurs sold Jennings to which club?

a) Chelsea b) Arsenal c) Everton

7. Spurs thought Jennings was in his twilight, but he went on to play over 300 games for this club. Which manager sold him?

a) Terry Neil b) Keith Burkinshaw c) David Pleat

8. In his 23 year career how many games did Jennings play?

a) 922 b) 1,012 c) 1,095

9. In 1993 Jennings became the goalkeeping coach at Spurs at which manager's behest?

a) Christian Gross b) Ossie Ardiles c) Peter Shreeves

10. **How many times did Jennings win the FA Cup?**

    a) 0 b) 1 c) 2

Quiz 14: 1960's Transfers

1. **In 1964 Spurs signed Alan Mullery for £72,000 from which club?**

    a) Fulham b) Watford c) Crystal Palace

2. **In 1966 Mike England was signed from which club?**

    a) Man City b) Oldham c) Blackburn

3. **In 1968 which 33 year old was sold for £5,000 to Derby?**

    a) Roy McFarland b) Dave McKay c) Archie Gemill

4. **1968 saw the arrival of which player from Southampton who would go on to score 118 league goals for Spurs?**

    a) Jimmy Neighbour b) Keith Weller c) Martin Chivers

5. **In December 1964 Spurs signed Alan Gilzean from which club?**

    a) Dundee b) Dunfermline c) Celtic

6. **In 1964 Bill Nicholson paid which club £64,000 for Cyril Knowles?**

    a) Newcastle b) Sunderland c) Middlesbrough

7. **On the 20th June 1969 Bill Nicholson accepted an offer of £70,000 from QPR for which player?**

   a) Jimmy Greaves b) Terry Venables c) Jimmy Robertson

8. **In 1964 Spurs sold which club legend to Brighton?**

   a) Bobby Smith b) Danny Blanchflower c) Les Allen

9. **In 1968, after playing 116 league games, Frank Saul was sold to which club?**

   a) Brighton b) Bournemouth c) Southampton

10. **In October 1968 Jimmy Robertson joined which club after playing 157 league games for Spurs?**

    a) Chelsea b) Man Utd c) Arsenal

Quiz 15: 1970's Transfers

1. **In March 1970 Spurs signed which World Cup winner?**

   a) Alan Ball b) George Cohen c) Martin Peters

2. **In 1971 Spurs bought Ralph Coates, who went on to play over 300 games for them, from which club?**

   a) Burnley b) Oldham c) Stockport

3. **In 1972 Spurs sold a player to Fulham who was the first England player to be sent off. He wasn't sold because of this but who was he?**

   a) Cyril Knowles b) Alan Mullery c) Martin Chivers

4. **In 1976 which club did Spurs sell Jimmy Neighbour to for £75,000?**

   a) Fulham b) Leicester c) Norwich

5. **In 1979 Spurs paid £300,000 to Coventry for the services of a player who would become a manager of the Welsh national team. Who was he?**

   a) Terry Yorath b) Bobby Gould c) Mike England

6. **In 1978 World Cup winner Ossie Ardiles was signed and stayed for 10 years. Which manager signed him?**

   a) David Pleat b) Terry Neill c) Keith Burkinshaw

7. **At the same time the club also signed Ricky Villa. What nationality was he?**

   a) Uruguayan b) Argentinian c) Spanish

8. **In 1976 Spurs signed a player for £400,000 from Crystal Palace who would at one stage of his career be a caretaker manager of England. Who was he?**

   a) Howard Wilkinson b) Chris Hughton c) Peter Taylor

9. **In 1975 Spurs signed a player for £25,000 from Bangor. The highlight of his career was scoring for Northern Ireland and beating the hosts Spain in the 1982 World Cup. Who was he?**

   a) Tony Galvin b) Gerry Armstrong c) Jimmy Holmes

10. **In 1976, after 278 league games in which he scored 118 goals, who did Spurs sell Martin Chivers to?**

    a) Norwich b) Southampton c) Servette

Quiz 16: 1980's Transfers

1. **In 1980 Spurs signed Steve Archibald who would go on to play 189 games for them and scored 77 times. Which club did Spurs pay £800,000 to sign him from?**

   a) Celtic b) Rangers c) Aberdeen

2. **In 1980 Spurs also bought a player for £650,000 from Stoke who would form a successful partnership with Archibald. Who was he?**

   a) Mark Falco b) Garth Crooks c) Micky Hazard

3. **In 1981 Spurs paid Liverpool £300,000 for a player who played 61 times for England. Who was he?**

   a) Ray Clemence b) Terry McDermott c) Phil Neal

4. **In 1988 Ossie Ardiles left Spurs and joined which club?**

   a) Monaco b) Marseille c) Blackburn

5. **In July 1989 Spurs signed Gary Lineker for £1.1m from which club?**

   a) Barcelona b) Leicester c) Everton

6. **On the 1st July 1989 Spurs sold Chris Waddle for £4.5m to which club?**

   a) Monaco b) Marseille c) PSG

7. **Spurs paid a record British transfer fee for Paul Gascoigne from Newcastle in 1988. How much did they pay?**

   a) £1.1m b) £2.2m c) £4.4m

8. **On the 19th June 1985 Spurs paid West Ham £400,000 for a player that would go on to play 370 games for the club scoring 28 goals. Who was the player?**

   a) Paul Allen b) Clive Allen c) Neil Ruddock

9. **In December 1986 David Pleat paid £650,000 for a player from Notts Forest. Who was he?**

   a) John Robertson b) Willie Young c) Steve Hodge

10. **In 1988 Erik Thorstvedt was signed and went on to play 218 games for the club. Which country was he born in?**

    a) Norway b) Sweden c) Finland

Quiz 17: 1990's Transfers

1. **In August 1992 Spurs signed Teddy Sheringham for £2.1m. The previous week he had scored the first ever live goal shown on Sky Sports against Liverpool. Which club was he signed from?**

   a) Millwall b) Portsmouth c) Notts Forest

2. **Spurs signed a player from Portsmouth for £1.75m in 1992. He became known as 'sicknote' despite which he still managed to play 358 games for the club. Who was he?**

   a) Justin Edinburgh b) Darren Anderton c) Stephen Carr

3. **January 1994 saw the arrival of Ronny Rosenthal from which club?**

   a) Everton b) West Ham c) Liverpool

4. **On the 6th October 1995 Spurs signed Ruel Fox for £4.25m. Which national team did he play for?**

   a) St Kitts b) Montserrat c) Bermuda

5. **In 1994 Spurs signed Jurgen Klinsmann. Which manager signed him?**

   a) Gerry Francis b) Christian Gross c) Ossie Ardiles

6. **In June 1995 Nick Barmby was sold to which club for £5.25m, becoming his new club's record signing at the time?**

   a) Newcastle b) Sunderland c) Middlesbrough

7. **July 1997 saw the arrival of David Ginola from Newcastle and he would go on to win the PFA Footballer of the Year with Spurs. What was the transfer fee?**

   a) Free b) £2.5m c) £5m

8. **1997 also saw the arrival of another player from Newcastle for £6m. Who was he?**

   a) Mauricio Taricco b) Tim Sherwood c) Les Ferdinand

9. **Pat Van Den Hauwe was sold to Millwall in 1993 after 145 games for the club. Which national team did he play for?**

   a) Belgium b) Netherlands c) Wales

10. **David Howells spent 12 years at Spurs playing 335 games for the club. In 1998 he was transferred to which club?**

    a) Southampton b) Bournemouth c) Portsmouth

Quiz 18: 2000's Transfers

1. **In May 2001 Spurs signed Gus Poyet for £2.1m from Chelsea. What nationality is he?**

   a) Argentinian b) Spanish c) Uruguayan

2. **Leeds were forced to sell players due to their financial crisis. One arrived at Spurs with a transfer fee of £7m in 2002. He went on to play 306 games for the club. Who was he?**

   a) Darren Bent b) Robbie Keane c) Jermaine Defoe

3. **On the 15th June 2005 another refugee from the Leeds crisis arrived and stayed for 10 years playing 364 games. Who was this?**

   a) Pascal Chimbonda b) Mido c) Aaron Lennon

4. **In March 2001 Dean Richards was signed from Southampton for £8.1m. He never fulfilled his potential due to injuries and illness, but which manager signed him?**

   a) George Graham b) Glenn Hoddle c) Jacques Santini

5. **Which team did Spurs sign Michael Dawson from on the 31st January 2005?**

   a) Notts Forest b) Hull c) Sheffield United

6. **In April 2008 Spurs agreed terms with Dinamo Zagreb for the signing of Luca Modric. What was the fee?**

   a) £10.5m b) £16.5m c) £22.5m

7. **The fee paid for Modric equalled the club record transfer fee. This was for a player who was signed on the 27th June 2007. Which player was this?**

   a) Dimitar Berbatov b) Jonathan Woodgate c) Darren Bent

8. **On the 27th July 2009 Spurs signed Peter Crouch for £10m from which club?**

   a) Portsmouth b) Liverpool c) Southampton

9. **On the 22nd July 2009 Spurs signed Kyle Walker from which club?**

   a) Leeds b) Oldham c) Sheffield United

10. **On the 25th May 2007 Gareth Bale was signed for an initial £5m rising to £10m on appearances from which club?**

    a) Cardiff b) Southampton c) Bristol City

Quiz 19: 2010+ Transfers

1. **On the 25th July 2007 Danny Rose was signed from which Division 1 club?**

   a) Brentford b) Oldham c) Leeds United

2. **Emmanuel Adebayor was signed in 2011 and went on to score 42 goals in 113 games for the club. What country was he born in and represented?**

   a) Ghana b) Togo c) Nigeria

3. **On the 29th August 2012 Spurs triggered a clause in Moussa Dembele's contract with Fulham to enable him**

to transfer. How much did they have to offer to trigger the clause?

a) £15m b) £20m c) £25m

4. **Spurs signed Toby Alderweireld in 2015 from which club?**

   a) Real Madrid b) Atletico Madrid c) Southampton

5. **Alderweireld joined Spurs and renewed a partnership with Jan Vertonghen. Which previous club had they been teammates?**

   a) Ajax b) Bayern Munich c) Seville

6. **Gareth Bale was sold to Real Madrid for a world record transfer at the time. How much did Madrid have to pay Spurs?**

   a) £78m b) 85m c) £96m

7. **On the 30th August 2013 Spurs set a then record transfer for the club when they bought Erik Lamela from which club?**

   a) Roma b) Lazio c) Napoli

8. **2015 saw Dele Ali arrive after a transfer from which club?**

   a) Peterborough b) Northampton c) MK Dons

9. **Eric Dier was signed in 2015 from which club?**

   a) Everton b) Birmingham c) Sport CP

10. **On the 28th August 2015 which club did Spurs pay £22m for Son Heung-Min?**

    a) Hamburg b) Bayer Leverkusen c) Dortmund

Quiz 20: White Hart Lane

1. **What year did Tottenham move to White Hart Lane?**

   a) 1892 b) 1899 c) 1902

2. **What was the ground previously used for?**

   a) An allotment b) Shooting range for military c) A nursery

3. **The first game was a friendly against Notts County and attracted a gate of 5,000 to watch. What were the gate receipts?**

   a) £115 b) £215 c) £315

4. **In 1905 in order to expand the facilities the club bought the freehold of the ground for how much?**

   a) £246 b) £2,890 c) £8,950

5. **The record gate at White Hart Lane was an FA Cup tie on the 5th March 1938 against Sunderland. How many spectators were there?**

   a) 62,535 b) 75,038 c) 84,198

6. **The 14th May 2017 saw the last game at White Hart Lane before the new stadium was constructed. Who were the opponents?**

   a) Man Utd b) Arsenal c) Liverpool

7. **One of the reasons for a new ground was that the ground capacity was well behind other similar clubs. What was the capacity allowed in their final season at White Hart Lane?**

   a) 36,300 b) 38,400 c) 40,600

8. **Spurs biggest win at the White Hart Lane came in February 1960 in an FA Cup tie against Crewe. What was the score?**

   a) 9 – 1 b) 11 – 4 c) 13 – 2

9. **How much did the new stadium cost?**

   a) £400m b) £750m c) £1 billion

10. **Who was the first player to score a Premier League goal at the new stadium?**

    a) Harry Kane b) Son Heung-min c) Moussa Sissoko

Quiz 21: Captains

1. **Who was captain during 2015 -?**

   a) Hugo Lloris b) Michael Vorm c) Christian Eriksen

2. **Who was captain during the 2014 – 15 season?**

   a) Jan Vertonghen b) Younes Kaboul c) Brad Friedel

3. **Who was captain during 2012 – 14?**

   a) Emmanuel Adebayor b) Aaron Lennon c) Michael Dawson

4. **Who was captain during 2005 -12?**

   a) Ledley King b) William Gallas c) Tom Huddlestone

5. **Who was captain during 2003 - 05 season?**

   a) Paul Robinson b) Robbie Keane c) Jaime Redknapp

6. **Who was captain during 2001 – 03?**

   a) Tim Sherwood b) Teddy Sheringham c) Gustavo Poyet

7. **Who was captain during 1998 - 2002?**

   a) Sol Campbell b) Les Ferdinand c) Darren Anderton

8. **Who was captain during 1987 – 98?**

   a) Jurgen Klinsmann b) Gary Mabbutt c) Colin Calderwood

9. **Who was captain during 1968 – 72?**

   a) Pat Jennings b) Joe Kinnear c) Allan Mullery

10. **Who was captain in the 1960 - 61 season?**

   a) Dave Mackay b) Bobby Smith c) Danny Blanchflower

Quiz 22: Players of The Year

1. **Who was the Tottenham Player of the Year in 2020?**

   a) Moussa Sissoko b) Harry Kane c) Heung-Min Son

2. **Who was the Tottenham Player of the Year in 2017?**

   a) Lucas Moura b) Christian Eriksen c) Dele Ali

3. **Who was the Tottenham Player of the Year in 2016?**

   a) Toby Alderweireld b) Jan Vertonghen c) Harry Kane

4. **Who was the Tottenham Player of the Year in 2012?**

   a) Gareth Bale b) Scott Parker c) Emmanuel Adebayor

5. **Who was the Tottenham Player of the Year in 2011?**

   a) William Gallas b) Luka Modric c) Kyle Walker

6. **Who was the Tottenham Player of the Year in 2010?**

   a) Danny Rose b) Michael Dawson c) Jonathan Woodgate

7. **Who was the Tottenham Player of the Year in 2003?**

   a) Robbie Keane b) Kasey Keller c) Christian Ziege

8. **Who was the Tottenham Player of the Year in 1997?**

   a) Les Ferdinand b) Sol Campbell c) David Ginola

9. **Who was the Tottenham Player of the Year in 1994?**

   a) Teddy Sheringham b) Darren Anderton c) Jurgen Klinsmann

10. **Who was the Tottenham Player of the Year in 1992?**

    a) Paul Gascoigne b) Garry Mabbutt c) Gary Lineker

Quiz 23: Managers

1. **Who was Tottenham manager from December 2013 to May 2014?**

   a) Andre Villas – Boas b) Clive Allen c) Tim Sherwood

2. **Who was Tottenham manager from October 2008 to June 2012?**

   a) Alex Inglethorpe b) Harry Redknapp c) Juande Ramos

3. **Martin Jol was appointed manager in 2004. What nationality was he?**

   a) Dutch b) German c) Danish

4. **Which manager did Martin Jol succeed at Tottenham?**

   a) David Pleat b) Jacques Santini c) Chris Hughton

5. **Who was the Tottenham manager from March 2001 to September 2003??**

   a) George Graham b) David Pleat c) Glenn Hoddle

6. **In November 1997 Spurs appointed Christian Gross as manager. What nationality is he?**

   a) German b) Swiss c) Danish

7. **Who was the Tottenham manager during 1994 – 97?**

   a) Steve Perryman b) Chris Hughton c) Gerry Francis

8. **Who was Tottenham manager during 1976 – 84?**

   a) Terry Neil b) Doug Livermore c) Keith Burkinshaw

9. **Peter Shreeves was manager from 1984 – 86. What nationality is he?**

   a) Scottish b) Welsh c) Northern Irish

10. **Who succeeded Bill Nicholson as manager in 1974?**

   a) David Pleat b) Terry Neil c) Doug Livermore

Quiz 24: First Division 1950 – 51 Champions

1. **How many times had Spurs won the First Division title prior to 1950 – 51?**

   a) 0 b) 1 c) 2

2. **Who came second in the league in 1950 – 51?**

   a) Newcastle b) Man Utd c) Blackpool

3. **Which future England manager played for Spurs this season?**

   a) Don Revie b) Joe Mercer c) Alf Ramsey

4. **Who scored the most goals for Spurs in 1950 – 51?**

   a) Les Bennett b) Alex Wright c) Sonny Walters

5. **Who was the Spurs manager for this season?**

   a) Joe Hulme b) Arthur Rowe c) Jimmy Anderson

6. **What was the style of play developed by this manager called?**

   a) Total football b) Push and run c) 4 – 4 - 2

7. **Who was the Spurs captain in 1950 – 51?**

   a) Ron Burgess b) Harry Clarke c) Eddie Baily

8. **Which future Spurs manager played for Spurs in the 1950 – 51 season?**

   a) Joe Mercer b) Bill Nicholson c) Alf Ramsey

9. **What record did Spurs set this year?**

   a) The most points in a First Division season b) The most goals scored in a Premier League season c) The first team to win the First and Second Division Championships in successive seasons

10. **What position did Spurs finish in the First Division in the season following their triumph?**

    a) 2nd b) Second to bottom c) Bottom

Quiz 25: First Division 1960 – 61 Champions

1. **In 1960 – 61 Spurs achieved the double of League and FA Cup. How many times had this been achieved before this season?**

   a) 0 b) 1 c) 2

2. **Who finished second in the league in 1960 – 61?**

   a) Man Utd b) Sheff Weds c) Burnley

3. **Who was the manager of the double winning team?**

   a) Bill Nicholson b) Jimmy Anderson c) Arthur Rowe

4. **Who was the leading goal scorer in 1960 – 61 for Spurs?**

   a) Jimmy Greaves b) Bobby Smith c) Les Allen

5. **Who was the double winning captain of Spurs this season?**

   a) Bobby Smith b) Dave MacKay c) Danny Blanchflower

6. **Who was the Spurs goalkeeper this season?**

   a) John Hollowbread b) Bill Brown c) Peter Baker

7. **How many league goals did Spurs score in the 1960 – 61 season?**

   a) 87 b) 98 c) 115

8. **Which player in 1960 - 61 had a son who scored 60 league goals for Spurs in later years?**

   a) Les Allen b) John White c) Bobby Smith

9. **How many Scottish players were used by Spurs during the season?**

   a) 2 b) 3 c) 4

10. **Where did Spurs finish in the following season in the league?**

    a) 3rd b) 16th c) 21st

Quiz 26: FA Cup 1960 – 61 Winner

1. **Who were the FA Cup defending champions in the 1960 – 61 competition?**

   a) Wolves b) Man Utd c) Liverpool

2. **How many times had Spurs won the FA Cup prior to their success in the 1960 – 61 competition?**

   a) 0 b) 1 c) 2

3. **Who did Spurs beat in the 1960 – 61 final?**

   a) Leicester b) Blackpool c) Blackburn

4. **What was the score that Spurs won by?**

   a) 1 – 0 b) 2 – 0 c) 3 – 0

5. **Which player in the Leicester team would become captain of Arsenal?**

   a) Don Howe b) George Eastham c) Frank McClintock

6. **Spurs were playing against a future World Cup winner in the final. Who was he?**

   a) Gordon Banks b) George Cohen c) Ray Wilson

7. **Who did Spurs beat in the semi-final of 1960 – 61?**

   a) Sunderland b) Burnley c) Sheffield Wednesday

8. **In the other semi-final how long did it take for the first goal to be scored?**

   a) 22 seconds b) 36 seconds c) 257 minutes

9. **Bobby Smith scored a goal in the final, but who else scored for Spurs?**

   a) Les Allen b) Terry Dyson c) John White

10. **Who was Spurs leading goal scorer in the 1960 – 61 FA Cup competition?**

    a) Les Allen b) Cliff Jones c) Bobby Smith

Quiz 27: UEFA Cup 1971 – 72 Winner

1. **This was the inaugural year of the UEFA Cup. Which competition did it replace?**

   a) UEFA Intertoto Cup b) Inter Cities Fairs Cup c) Intercontinental Cup

2. **Spurs beat Keflavik in the first round of the 1971 - 72 competition. What was the aggregate score?**

   a) 11 – 1 b) 15 – 1 c) 19 -1

3. **Which country are Keflavik from?**

   a) Iceland b) Norway c) Albania

4. **Who did Spurs beat in the final?**

   a) Atlctico Madrid b) Leeds c) Wolves

5. **Who was the Spurs captain for the tie?**

   a) Mike England b) Joe Kinnear c) Allan Mullery

6. **There was one player for the Republic of Ireland who played in the final. Who was he?**

   a) Derek Dougan b) Joe Kinnear c) Danny Hegan

7. **Which player scored the most goals for Spurs in the competition?**

   a) Alan Gilzean b) Alan Mullery c) Martin Chivers

8. **Who did Spurs beat in the semi-final with a 3 – 2 aggregate victory?**

   a) AC Milan b) Real Madrid c) Bayern Munich

9. **In the following season's UEFA Cup Spurs were beaten on away goals in the semi -final by the eventual winner. Which team won the competition in 1972 – 73?**

   a) Twente b) Dortmund c) Liverpool

10. **Who was the Spurs manager during the 1971 – 72 UEFA Cup triumph?**

    a) Bill Nicholson b) Jack Burkinshaw c) Terry Neill

Quiz 28: FA Cup 1990 – 91 Winner

1. **Who was the Spurs manager during the 1990 – 91 FA Cup triumph?**

   a) Peter Shreeves b) Terry Venables c) Osvaldo Ardiles

2. **Who did Spurs meet in the final?**

   a) West Ham b) Arsenal c) Notts Forest

3. **Who was the Spurs captain in the final?**

   a) Gary Mabbutt b) Gary Lineker c) Justin Edinburgh

4. **Spurs won the final 2 -1. Who scored the winning goal for Spurs?**

   a) Gary Lineker b) Paul Allen c) Des Walker

5. **Including this victory how many times have Spurs won the FA Cup?**

   a) 6 b) 7 c) 8

6. **In the first half Spurs had a penalty which Lineker took and was saved. It was saved by Mark Crossley and was only the second to be saved in an FA Cup Final at Wembley. Who saved the first?**

   a) Bert Trautmann b) Dave Beasant c) Alex Stepney

7. **Paul Gascoigne received a career changing injury early in the game. Who replaced him from the bench?**

   a) Nayim b) Paul Walsh c) Vinny Samways

8. **Who was the Spurs goalkeeper?**

   a) Ian Walker b) Kasey Keller c) Erik Thorstvedt

9. **Who did Arsenal beat in the semi-final in 1990 - 91?**

   a) Arsenal b) West Ham c) Chelsea

10. **Who was the top goal scorer in the 1990 – 91 FA Cup competition?**

    a) Gary Lineker b) Paul Allen c) Paul Gascoigne

Quiz 29: 1983 – 84 UEFA Cup Winner

1. **Who did Spurs play in the 1984 UEFA Cup final?**

   a) Ajax b) Anderlecht c) Malmo

2. **Who did Spurs beat in the semi-final?**

   a) Spartak Moscow b) Austria Wien c) Hajduk Split

3. **Anderlecht won the semi-final against Notts Forest in what was subsequently proven to be scandalous fashion. What did Anderlecht do?**

   a) Put laxatives in Notts Forest biscuits b) Played music all night outside the Forest hotel c) Bribed the referee

4. **How did Spurs win the final?**

   a) Toss of a coin b) Penalties c) Extra time in the second leg

5. **Who was the Spurs captain for the final?**

   a) Steve Perryman b) Gary Mabbutt c) Chris Hughton

6. **In their defense of the UEFA Cup in the 1984 – 85 season they lost in the quarter-finals to which team?**

   a) Barcelona b) PSG c) Real Madrid

7. **Who was the Spurs goalkeeper in the final?**

   a) Ray Clemence b) Tony Parkes c) Ian Walker

8. **Who was the only Scottish player to have played in the final for Spurs?**

   a) Steve Archibald b) Alan Brazil c) Richard Gough

9. **Who was the Spurs manager for the final?**

   a) Peter Shreeves b) David Pleat c) Keith Burkinshaw

10. **In the final Spurs played against someone who would subsequently become their Director of Football. Who was he?**

    a) Michel de Groote b) Frank Arnesen c) Enzo Scifo

Quiz 30: 1966 – 67 FA Cup Winner

1. **Who did Spurs play in the 1967 FA Cup Final?**

   a) West Brom b) Liverpool c) Chelsea

2. **What was the score by which Spurs won the final?**

   a) 2 – 0 b) 2 – 1 c) 3 – 1

3. **Who were the defending FA Cup winners in 1966 – 67?**

   a) Everton b) Liverpool c) Sheffield Wednesday

4. **The 1967 final was the first what?**

   a) To use red and yellow cards b) To use substitutes c) All London final

5. **Who did Spurs beat in the semi-final?**

   a) Leeds b) Notts Forest c) Man City

6. **Who was the Spurs captain in the final?**

   a) Dave MacKay b) Terry Venables c) Allan Mullery

7. **Two players in the final were in the 1966 England World Cup Squad. One was Jimmy Greaves, who was the other?**

   a) Allan Mullery b) Tony Hateley c) Peter Bonetti

8. **Who scored the goals for Spurs?**

   a) Robertson and Saul b) Gilzean and Greaves c) Venables

and England

9. **Who was Spurs goalkeeper?**

   a) Bill Brown b) Pat Jennings c) Joe Corrigan

10. **How many players from the double winning squad of 1960 – 61 played in the winning FA Cup team of 1967?**

   a) 1 b) 2 c) 3

Quiz 31: 2007 –08 League Cup Winner

1. **Who sponsored the League Cup this season?**

   a) Carling b) Worthington c) Capital One

2. **Who were the finalists that Spurs beat in 2007 – 08?**

   a) Arsenal b) Chelsea c) Watford

3. **Who scored the winning goal for Spurs in extra time?**

   a) Keane b) Berbatov c) Woodgate

4. **Who did Spurs beat 6 – 2 on aggregate in the semi-final?**

   a) Arsenal b) Man Utd c) Liverpool

5. **Who was the Spurs manager for the game?**

   a) Harry Redknapp b) Juande Ramos c) Martin Jol

6. **Spurs fielded a player from the Ivory Coast in the final. Which one was he?**

   a) Malbranque b) Chimbonda c) Zakora

7. **Who was Spurs goalkeeper for the game?**

   a) Paul Robinson b) Radek Cerny c) Heurelho Gomes

8. **Who was the Spurs captain in the final?**

   a) Robbie Keane b) Tom Huddlestone c) Ledley King

9. **Dimitar Berbatov scored with a penalty following a handball. Who was it that handled the ball?**

   a) Nicolas Anelka b) Wayne Bridge c) John Terry

10. **Teemu Tainio came off the bench to play for Spurs. What nationality is he?**

    a) Finland b) Norway c) Sweden

Quiz 32: Son Heung-Min

1. **What year was Son born?**

   a) 1991 b) 1992 c) 1993

2. **Which German team was his first European club?**

   a) Hamburg b) Bayern Munich c) Bayer Leverkusen

3. **Son is fluent in German. How did he learn the language?**

   a) War films b) An online course c) Watching SpongeBob SquarePants

4. **On the 28th August 2015 Spurs bought Son from which club?**

   a) Hamburg b) Bayern Munich c) Bayer Leverkusen

5. **How much did Spurs pay for him?**

   a) £15m b) £22m c) £30m

6. **How was Son able to avoid two years National Service in Korea?**

   a) He gave the state one year's salary b) He gave up South Korean citizenship c) He was in the 2018 Korean team that won the gold at the Asian games

7. **In September 2020 Son scored 4 goals all with assists from Kane. Who were the opponents?**

   a) Fulham b) Southampton c) Sheffield United

8. **What season did he win the BBC Goal of the Season?**

   a) 2017 – 18 b) 2018 – 19 c) 2019 – 20

9. **On the 2nd January 2021 Son scored his 100th goal for Tottenham against which team?**

   a) Leeds b) West Ham c) Burnley

10. **Who does Son have a sponsorship deal with?**

    a) Nike b) Adidas c) Samsung

Quiz 33: Danny Blanchflower

1. **Where was Blanchflower born?**

   a) Belfast b) Dublin c) Cardiff

2. **Which branch of the services did he join in 1943?**

   a) Navy b) Army c) RAF

3. **His first club was Glentoran but in 1949 he signed for which English club?**

   a) Aston Villa b) Barnsley c) Sheffield Wednesday

4. **In 1954 Blanchflower joined Spurs. How much did Spurs have to pay for him?**

   a) Free transfer b) £5,000 c) £30,000

5. **How many games did he play for Spurs?**

   a) 346 b) 382 c) 428

6. **Blanchflower was appointed the manager of which club in 1978?**

   a) Arsenal b) Aston Villa c) Chelsea

7. **Blanchflower was one of many signatories of a letter to the Times opposing what?**

   a) Drugs in sport b) Apartheid in sport c) Gambling

8. Blanchflower also refused to appear on which TV program?

a) This is your life b) Match of the Day c) Panorama

9. What was the name of Blanchflower's brother whose career was ended in injuries sustained in the Munich Air Crash?

a) Robert b) Dennis c) Jackie

10. How many trophies did Blanchflower win with Spurs?

a) 3 b) 4 c) 5

Quiz 34: Ledley King

1. What is King's middle name?

a) Bailey b) Bunsen c) Brenton

2. Which manager gave King his debut in the first team?

a) George Graham b) David Pleat c) Glenn Hoddle

3. His first goal for Spurs came in December 2000 in a 3 – 3 draw with Bradford City. What was unusual about it?

a) It was the 5,000th Premier League goal b) It was scored in 9.82 seconds c) It deflected off a beach ball

4. **How many games did King play for Spurs in his 14 years as a player at the club?**

   a) 323 b) 423 c) 523

5. **King was appointed as assistant coach to which manager?**

   a) Mauricio Pochettino b) Harry Redknapp c) Jose Mourinho

6. **How many times was Ledley King the Tottenham Player of the Year?**

   a) 0 b) 1 c) 2

7. **How many seasons was Ledley King the First team captain?**

   a) 5 b) 6 c) 7

8. **In 2011 a steel statue was erected of Ledley King. Where was it placed?**

   a) At White Hart Lane South Stand b) Lordship Recreation Ground, Tottenham c) Mile End Park

9. **What shirt number was King?**

   a) 26 b) 32 c) 39

10. **How many trophies did he win at Tottenham?**

   a) 0 b) 1 c) 2

Quiz 35: Cyril Knowles

1. **What was Knowles middle name?**

   a) George b) Barry c) Phillip

2. **What sport did Knowles' father, also called Cyril, play professionally?**

   a) Rugby League b) Cricket c) Tennis

3. **Which was Knowles' first professional club?**

   a) Leeds b) Hull c) Middlesbrough

4. **How much did Spurs pay for Knowles?**

   a) Free transfer b) £20,000 c) £45,000

5. **Before the 1973 League Cup Final a record was released, "Nice one Cyril", which was a reference to Knowles. Who released the record?**

   a) Cockerel Chorus b) Slade c) Mungo Jerry

6. **What position did Knowles play?**

   a) Right back b) Left back c) Centre half

7. **How many games did he play for Spurs?**

   a) 506 b) 543 c) 598

8. **How many games did he play for England?**

   a) 0 b) 4 c) 18

9. **How many trophies did he win during his time at Tottenham?**

   a) 4 b) 6 c) 8

10. **Cyril Knowles had a younger brother called Peter who played for Wolves. He retired at aged 24 for what reason?**

    a) He became a successful pop singer b) He was in prison c) He became a Jehovah's Witness

Quiz 36: Hugo Lloris

1. **Lloris was born in Nice, France. What body of water is Nice on?**

   a) Bay of Biscay b) English Channel c) Mediterranean Sea

2. **What year was Lloris born?**

   a) 1986 b) 1984 c) 1982

3. **What other sport was he in the national rankings for before he committed to football?**

   a) Rugby Union b) Tennis c) Water Polo

4. **Which club did Spurs buy Lloris from?**

   a) Lyon b) Nice c) Monaco

5. **Lloris' first Premier League game was in October 2012. He displaced which keeper?**

   a) Paul Robinson b) Heurelho Gomes c) Brad Friedel

6. **Lloris was in the 2014 World Cup in Brazil with the French team. At what stage were France knocked out of the tournament?**

   a) Quarter-Finals b) Semi-Finals c) The Final

7. **Lloris won the World Cup with France in 2018. Who did France beat in the semi-final?**

   a) Belgium b) Brazil c) Croatia

8. **Also, in 2018 he was voted runner up in the Best Fifa Goalkeeper Award. Who was the best goalkeeper?**

   a) Allison b) Ederson c) Courtois

9. **What year was Lloris appointed the Tottenham captain?**

   a) 2014 – 15 b) 2015 – 16 c) 2016 – 17

10. **The highest Premier League finish since Lloris was at the club was 2nd. Which season was this?**

    a) 2016 – 17 b) 2017 – 18 c) 2018 - 19

Quiz 37: Chris Hughton

1. **What year was Chris Hughton born?**

   a) 1958 b) 1960 c) 1962

2. **What four year apprenticeship did he complete before signing for Spurs?**

   a) Lift engineer b) Welder c) Artificial Intelligence Systems Analyst

3. **What position did he play?**

   a) Right back b) Left back c) Midfield

4. **Which manager gave him his debut at Spurs?**

   a) Peter Shreeves b) David Pleat c) Keith Burkinshaw

5. **How many games did he play for Spurs?**

   a) 294 b) 347 c) 398

6. **Which country did he represent?**

   a) Republic of Ireland b) Northern Ireland c) Wales

7. **In November 1990 Hughton left Spurs to play for which club?**

   a) Crystal Palace b) Norwich C) West Ham

8. **How many trophies did he win playing for Spurs?**

   a) 0 b) 2 c) 4

9. **He became a coach at Tottenham from June 1993 to October 2007. How many different Tottenham managers did he serve under during his time at Tottenham?**

   a) 9 b) 12 c) 15

10. **Which club was his first managerial position?**

    a) Newcastle b) Norwich c) Crystal Palace

Quiz 38: Jermain Defoe

1. **What is Defoe's middle name?**

   a) Colin b) Philip c) David

2. **Early on he joined Senrab, which is a Sunday League team based at Wanstead Flats. Which other player has also played for Senrab?**

   a) Ledley King b) John Terry c) Ashley Cole

3. **Which club gave him his professional debut?**

   a) Portsmouth b) West Ham c) Bournemouth

4. **Defoe is sixth in the list of all time goal scorers for Spurs. How many did he get in his 363 games for the club?**

   a) 123 b) 133 c) 143

5. **How many seasons was Defoe Spurs leading Premier League goal scorer?**

   a) 1 b) 2 c) 3

6. **In January 2008 Spurs sold Defoe for £7.5m to which club?**

   a) Bournemouth b) Portsmouth c) Sunderland

7. **A year later Defoe returned to Spurs. How much was it reported that Spurs paid for his return?**

   a) £3.75m b) £7.5m c) £15.75m

8. **In 2013 Defoe started a charitable foundation called the 'Jermain Defoe Foundation'. What does the charity seek to support?**

   a) Young people b) Cats and dogs c) A hospice

9. **Which club was Defoe with when he scored his 300th career club goal?**

   a) Bournemouth b) Rangers c) Portsmouth

10. **How many times did Defoe play for England?**

    a) 37 b) 47 c) 57

Quiz 39: Jan Vertonghen

1. **Where was Vertonghen born?**

    a) Belgium b) Holland c) Germany

2. **Which was his first professional club?**

    a) Feyenoord b) Eindhoven c) Ajax

3. **How many Euros did Vertonghen cost Spurs when he joined them on the 8th July 2012?**

    a) €8 million b) €12 million c) €16 million

4. **Who was the Tottenham manager who signed Vertonghen?**

    a) Harry Redknapp b) Martin Jol c) Andre Villas-Boas

5. **In March 2013 he was named the Premier League Player of the Month, the second Belgian to be so named. Who was the first?**

    a) Christian Benteke b) Eden Hazard c) Marouane Fellaini

6. **How many games did Vertonghen play for Spurs?**

    a) 280 b) 315 c) 349

7. **At the end of the 2019 – 20 season Vertonghen became a free agent. Which club did he sign for?**

    a) Benfica b) Porto c) Seville

8. **What year was he the Tottenham Player of the Year?**

   a) 2016 b) 2017 c) 2018

9. **Vertonghen suffered a head injury is an accidental clash with Alderweireld which he says affected him for 9 months. Which team did he sustain the injury against?**

   a) Man Utd b) Ajax c) Liverpool

10. **Which former Spurs manager was his coach when he played for Ajax?**

    a) Martin Jol b) Jacques Santini c) Juande Ramos

Quiz 40: Martin Chivers

1. **What is Chivers' middle name?**

   a) Harcourt b) Harrison c) Hugo

2. **His first professional team was at his local club, which was?**

   a) Wolverhampton b) Exeter c) Southampton

3. **In January 1968 Bill Nicholson signed Chivers for Spurs. What was the transfer fee?**

   a) £12,000 b) £35,000 c) £125,000

4. How did Chivers find out he was being sold to Spurs?

a) A phone call from his mother b) A billboard down the High Street c) It was on the Nine O'clock News

5. How many seasons was Chivers the leading Spurs goal scorer?

a) 4 b) 5 c) 6

6. He scored 174 goals for Spurs. How many games did he play to get them?

a) 367 b) 423 c) 486

7. He was the leading Spurs goal scorer in European competitions with 22 goals for some time. Who eventually beat it?

a) Harry Kane b) Robbie Keane c) Jermain Defoe

8. In July 1976 Spurs sold Chivers on to Servette for £80,000. Which country are Servette from?

a) Switzerland b) Austria c) Belgium

9. How many caps did Chivers get for England?

a) 24 b) 44 c) 64

10. In 2009 Chivers produced an autobiography. What was it titled?

a) Anything is Possible b) I'll Tell You What… c) Big Chiv

Quiz 41: Alan Gilzean

1. **What year was Gilzean born?**

   a) 1928 b) 1938 c) 1948

2. **Which was his first professional club?**

   a) Dundee b) Aberdeen c) Rangers

3. **He played 190 league appearances for this team. How many league goals did he get?**

   a) 86 b) 123 c) 169

4. **In December 1964 he moved to Spurs. What was the transfer fee?**

   a) £35,500 b) £72,500 c) £84,500

5. **How many games did he play for Spurs?**

   a) 364 b) 405 c) 439

6. **How many seasons was Gilzean the leading goal scorer for Spurs?**

   a) 0 b) 2 c) 4

7. **How many international caps did Gilzean get?**

   a) 22 b) 42 c) 62

8. **What job did he take up on leaving football?**

   a) Funeral director b) Transport c) Electrician

9. **How many trophies did Gilzean win at Spurs?**

   a) 3 b) 5 c) 7

10. **Gilzean has an autobiography which was titled the name given to him by Spurs fans. What was it?**

    a) The King of White Hart Lane b) Slinky c) Killer

Quiz 42: Robbie Keane

1. **Where was Keane born?**

   a) Belfast b) Dublin c) Swansea

2. **What was his first professional club that he signed for just before his 16th birthday?**

   a) Coventry b) Leeds c) Wolves

3. **In July 2000 Keane was signed by Inter Milan for £13m. How many league games did he play for them?**

   a) 6 b) 60 c) 120

4. **In 2001 Keane joined Leeds for a fee of £12m. Who was the Leeds manager who signed him?**

   a) George Graham b) David O'Leary c) Terry Venables

5. **Keane has 146 international caps for the Republic of Ireland. Who is second to Keane in this list?**

   a) Kevin Kilbane b) John O'Shea c) Shay Given

6. **What was Keane's shirt number at Tottenham?**

   a) 8 b) 10 c) 12

7. **In December 2005 Keane was involved in a training ground scrap with which Tottenham teammate?**

   a) Edgar Davids b) Jermaine Jenas c) Aaron Lennon

8. **Which American club did Keane play for?**

   a) Colorado Rapids b) San Jose Earthquakes c) LA Galaxy

9. **On the 4th August 2017 Keane joined Indian Super League team ATK. Which former Tottenham teammate was head coach?**

   a) Teddy Sheringham b) Gus Poyet c) Mido

10. **How many times was he the Tottenham Hotspur Player of the Year?**

   a) 1 b) 2 c)3

Quiz 43: Christian Eriksen

1. **What year was Eriksen born?**

   a) 1991 b) 1992 c) 1993

2. **On the 30th August 2013 Eriksen joined Spurs from which club?**

   a) Ajax b) Monaco c) Dortmund

3. **On this same day Spurs also acquired another player. Who was he?**

   a) Roberto Soldado b) Eric Dier c) Erik Lamela

4. **Who was Spurs manager when Eriksen was signed?**

   a) Harry Redknapp b) Andre Villas-Boas c) Tim Sherwood

5. **On the 28th January 2020 Eriksen left Spurs and signed for which club?**

   a) Roma b) Juventus c) Inter Milan

6. **He made his debut for this club the following day by coming on as a substitute for who?**

   a) Alexis Sanchez b) Victor Moses c) Ashley Young

7. **How many games did Eriksen play for Spurs?**

   a) 256 b) 287 c) 305

8. **What number shirt did Eriksen wear at Spurs?**

   a) 13 b) 23 c) 33

9. **Eriksen's sister plays club football and been picked for the national team. What is her name?**

   a) Freja b) Karla c) Louise

10. **How many times was Christian Eriksen the Tottenham Player of the Year?**

    a) 1 b) 2 c) 3

Quiz 44: Aaron Lennon

1. **What is Lennon's middle name?**

   a) Justin b) Piers c) Luther

2. **When he joined Leeds Academy, he was the youngest player at the time to have his boots sponsored. How old was he?**

   a) 12 b) 14 c) 16

3. **His debut in the Premier League for Leeds also made him the youngest player, at the time, to appear in the Premier League. How old was he?**

   a) 16 years 42 days b) 16 years 84 days c) 16 years 129 days

4. **Following Leeds' well documented financial problems Lennon was transferred to Spurs on the 15th June 2005. What was the fee that Leeds received?**

   a) £1m b) £5m c) £10m

5. **Which Spurs manager signed him?**

   a) Jacques Santini b) Martin Jol c) Juande Ramos

6. **How many games did he play for Spurs?**

   a) 328 b) 347 c) 364

7. **In 2015 he was sold to Everton. What was the reported transfer fee?**

   a) £4.5m b) £6.5m c) £8.5m

8. **On the 2nd September 2020 he signed for Kayserispor. Which country are they from?**

   a) Germany b) Turkey c) Malta

9. **How many full England caps did Lennon get?**

   a) 11 b) 21 c) 31

10. **What was the one major trophy that Lennon won with Spurs?**

    a) League Cup b) FA Cup c) Europa Cup

Quiz 45: Darren Anderton

1. **What year was Anderton born?**

   a) 1968 b) 1970 c) 1972

2. **What was Anderton's first professional club?**

   a) Southampton b) Portsmouth c) Bournemouth

3. **In 1992 he joined Tottenham for what transfer fee?**

   a) £1.75m b) £3.5m c) £6.25m

4. **What was Anderton's nickname?**

   a) Handy b) The Ghost c) Sicknote

5. **Anderton was with Spurs from 1992 – 2004. How many games did he play during this period with Spurs?**

   a) 384 b) 423 c) 464

6. **In 2004 Anderton left on a free transfer to go to which club?**

   a) Wolves b) Southampton c) Birmingham

7. **Which Spurs manager sold Anderton?**

   a) David Pleat b) Jacques Santini c) Martin Jol

8. **Anderton played 18 league games in Division 2 (fourth tier) with which club?**

   a) Reading b) Bournemouth c) Brighton

9. **Anderton was the Tottenham Player of the Year once. Which year was it?**

   a) 1993 b) 1995 c) 1997

10. **How many games did Anderton play for England?**

    a) 24 b) 26 c) 30

Quiz 46: Bobby Smith

1. **What year was Bobby Smith born?**

   a) 1923 b) 1933 c) 1943

2. **He was born in Yorkshire, but his first professional club was a London club. Which one?**

   a) Chelsea b) Arsenal c) Watford

3. **In December 1955 he was transferred to Tottenham. What was the transfer fee?**

   a) £1,000 b) £8,000 c) £18,000

4. **What was his weekly wage when he joined Spurs?**

   a) £17/week b) £32/week c) £140/week

5. **He played a total of 317 games for Spurs. How many goals did he get in those games?**

    a) 145 b) 187 c) 208

6. **In 1964 Smith left Spurs for which club?**

    a) Portsmouth b) Brighton c) Bournemouth

7. **What job did he do after leaving football?**

    a) Painter and decorator b) Pop singer c) Pig farmer

8. **Smith was part of the 1954 – 55 Championship winning Chelsea squad. What did Smith say that Chelsea sent every member of the squad at Christmas?**

    a) A season ticket b) A Christmas hamper c) £1500

9. **How many games did Smith play for England?**

    a) 15 b) 30 c) 45

10. **In 1999 his 1961 FA Cup winners medal was stolen from his house. It was subsequently sold at auction without Smith's knowledge. How much did it sell for?**

    a) £1,200 b) £5,600 c) £11,200

Quiz 47: Michael Dawson

1. **What is Dawson's middle name?**

   a) Phillip b) Andrew c) Richard

2. **What was Dawson's first professional club?**

   a) Notts Forest b) Sheffield Wednesday c) Leeds

3. **Dawson and another player were transferred to Spurs for a combined fee of £8m. Who was the other player?**

   a) Sean Davies b) Calum Davenport c) Andy Reid

4. **How many games did he play for Spurs?**

   a) 246 b) 324 c) 416

5. **How many goals did he score for Spurs?**

   a) 5 b) 8 c) 10

6. **How many seasons was Michael Dawson captain of Spurs for?**

   a) 2 b) 3 c) 4

7. **On the 26th August 2014 Dawson left Spurs for which club?**

   a) Hull b) Sheff Utd c) Leeds

8. **He made his international debut against Hungary in 2010. How many games did he play for England?**

   a) 1 b) 4 c) 12

9. **What year was Dawson the Tottenham Player of the Year?**

   a) 2009 – 10 b) 2010 – 11 c) 2011 – 12

10. **Dawson became captain of Spurs midway through the 2009 – 10 season when who left the club?**

    a) Ledley King b) Younes Kaboul c) Robbie Keane

Quiz 48: Jurgen Klinsmann

1. **Klinsmann has served an apprenticeship in what profession?**

   a) Tailor b) Baker c) Candle stick maker

2. **Klinsmann was part of the German team that won the 1990 World Cup. Who did they beat in the final?**

   a) Argentina b) Italy c) Spain

3. **He was signed in July 1994 by Spurs from which club?**

   a) Inter Milan b) Monaco c) Bayern Munich

4. **How much was the transfer fee?**

   a) Free transfer b) £2 million c) £10 million

5. **What position did Spurs finish in the Premier League in the 1994 – 95 season?**

   a) 2nd b) 4th c) 7th

6. **He was the national coach of Germany from 2004 to 2006. What other national team has he managed?**

   a) Qatar b) Austria c) USA

7. **How many games did Klinsmann play for Spurs?**

   a) 54 b) 68 c) 75

8. **How many goals did he get in those games for Spurs?**

   a) 18 b) 28 c) 38

9. **Klinsmann competed in the 1988 Summer Olympics for West Germany. What medal did he win?**

   a) Gold b) Silver c) Bronze

10. **He rejoined Spurs in the 1997 – 98 season and in May 1998 scored 4 goals in a game against which team?**

    a) Wimbledon b) Everton c) Derby

Quiz 49: Osvaldo Ardiles

1. **What nationality is Ardiles?**

   a) Uruguayan b) Columbian c) Argentinian

2. **Which manager signed Ardiles for Spurs?**

   a) Keith Burkinshaw b) Peter Shreeves c) David Pleat

3. **Which other overseas player was also signed at the same time as Ardiles?**

   a) Daniel Passarella b) Ricardo Villa c) Mario Kempes

4. **As was the fashion in those days Ardiles, and the rest of the Tottenham team, produced a record entitled 'Ossie's Dream'. Who did they collaborate with?**

   a) Bananarama b) Slade c) Chas & Dave

5. **In 1982 Ardiles left Spurs on loan to play for PSG for a season. Why did he go?**

   a) A dip in form b) The Falklands War c) Fell out with the manager

6. **In 1988 he left Spurs after a decade and joined which club?**

   a) Monaco b) PSG c) Blackburn

7. **Which club did he begin his management career at?**

   a) Swindon b) West Brom c) Newcastle

8. **Ardiles won the play offs with this club to get into the First Division (top tier). However, they didn't get promoted. Why was this?**

   a) Played an illegal player in the play offs b) The size of the First Division was reduced from 22 to 20 clubs c) Financial irregularities

9. **He became manager of Tottenham in 1993 but it didn't go well, and he was sacked in October 1994. Who replaced him as the permanent Spurs manager?**

   a) Cristian Gross b) Gerry Francis c) Glenn Hoddle

10. **Ardiles and Vilas were injured in a car crash filming for a documentary. Where did the crash happen?**

    a) USA b) Argentina c) The Falkland Islands

Quiz 50: Miscellaneous

1. **Jimmy Greaves and Harry Kane are the two leading scorers for Spurs, but who is third in the all-time list?**

   a) Bobby Smith b) Martin Chivers c) Cliff Jones

2. **Who was nicknamed 'The Rocket'?**

   a) Jimmy Robertson b) Ronnie Rosenthal c) Gerry Armstrong

3. **When Gary Lineker left Spurs in 1992 which country did he go to play in?**

   a) USA b) Qatar c) Japan

4. **Jason Cundy scored a single league goal for Spurs which was against Ipswich in the 1992 – 93 season. What was memorable about it?**

   a) It deflected in off the referee b) It was scored from the halfway line c) The goalkeeper was tying his shoelaces

5. **Tottenham won the FA Cup for the first time in 1901 after a replay against Sheffield United. What was unusual about this win?**

   a) Spurs were a non-league club b) It was watched by a record crowd at the time c) A Spurs player scored in every round

6. **In 1986 in Ossie Ardiles' testimonial against Inter Milan who wore the Spurs number 10 shirt?**

   a) George Best b) Pele c) Maradona

7. **Who has scored the most goals in a single season for Spurs?**

   a) Jimmy Greaves b) Clive Allen c) Gary Lineker

8. **The club was named after Harry Hotspur. What was Harry Hotspur's real name?**

   a) Sir Henry Percy b) Sir George Spurn c) Sir Harold

Bolingbroke

9. **What is Spurs' Latin motto?**

   a) Ad Astra per aspera b) Quis Audet Vincit c) Audere Est Facere

10. **What nationality is Erik Lamela?**

    a) Uruguayan b) Peruvian c) Argentinian

11. **Who were the first commercial club sponsor to appear on a Tottenham shirt?**

    a) Thompson b) Holsten c) Mansion

12. **How much are the current sponsor, AIA, alleged to be paying Spurs per year?**

    a) £8m b) £20m c) £40m

13. **What do AIA do?**

    a) Betting b) Insurance c) Brewery

14. **Tottenham was the first club to float on the Stock Exchange. Which year was this?**

    a) 1898 b) 1976 c) 1983

15. **What is the record attendance for a Tottenham game?**

    a) 73,451 b) 82, 639 c) 85,512

16. **Spurs record win was 13 – 2 in an FA Cup game in 1960 against which team?**

    a) Grimsby b) Crewe Alexandra c) Accrington Stanley

17. What season is the last one that Tottenham were relegated?

a) 1972 – 73 b) 1976 – 77 c) 1980 -81

18. In July 1998 Spurs signed Gary Lineker from which club?

a) Barcelona b) Everton c) Leicester

19. How many league goals did Lineker score for Spurs?

a) 43 b) 67 b) 82

20. John White was a member of the 1960 – 61 double winning team who died in tragic circumstances at the age of 27. How did he die?

a) Car crash b) Plane crash c) Lightening strike

21. In May 1992 Spurs signed Razor Ruddock for £750,000 from which club?

a) Southampton b) Millwall c) Swindon

22. Where was Lucas Moura born?

a) Spain b) Columbia c) Brazil

23. On the 28th November 2012 against Liverpool, a Tottenham player scored a goal, provided an assist and also scored an own goal. Who was the player?

a) David Bentley b) Gareth Bale c) Aaron Lennon

24. What nationality is Dimitar Berbatov?

a) Croatian b) Serbian c) Bulgarian

25. On the 17th March 2007 Paul Robinson scored a 95 yard goal for Spurs against which team?

a) Watford b) Fulham c) Everton

26. In July 1997 Spurs paid which club £2.5m for David Ginola?

a) Aston Villa b) Everton c) Newcastle

27. Who scored the first goal for Spurs in the Premier League in the 1992 – 93 season?

a) Darren Anderton b) Gordon Durie c) Teddy Sheringham

28. The new stadium is said to have the longest bar in the world. How long is it?

a) 56.4m b) 86.8m c) 98.3m

29. Eric Dier made his senior England debut on the 5th November 2015. Which other country approached him about playing for them?

a) Portugal b) Spain c) France

30. What is the highest finishing position in the Premier League for Spurs?

a) 2nd b) 3rd c) 4th

31. Tottenham played their first Premier League game at the new stadium on the 3rd April 2019, after much delay. Who were their opponents in this game?

a) Everton b) Arsenal c) Crystal Place

32. In 2021 cinch became Spurs' first 'Official Sleeve Partner'. What do cinch do?

a) Online car sales b) Overseas money transfers c) Sportswear sales

33. How many times have Spurs won the FA Cup?

a) 6 b) 7 c) 8

34. Who is the only Norwegian to have been the Tottenham Player of the Year?

a) Erik Thorstvedt b) Tore Andre Flo c) Steffan Iversen

35. Who is Spurs youngest goal scorer?

a) Stephen Carr b) Andy Turner c) Alfie Devine

36. Ted Croker was Secretary of the FA from 1973 – 89. Who is his grandson?

a) Joe Rodon b) Eric Dier c) Harry Winks

37. On December the 4th 1965 Frank Saul was sent off playing against Burnley for Spurs. What was unusual about this sending off?

a) He was sent off for swinging on the crossbar and breaking it b) It was a case of mistaken identity c) He was the first Spurs player to be sent off for 37 years

38. In May 2016 Spurs played at Chelsea and set a Premier League record. What was the record?

a) Spurs had a record 23 corners b) Spurs had 9 players booked c) No shots at all

39. How many times was Mauricio Pochettino sent off as a player?

a) 0 b) 3 c) 13

40. Who scored the 10,000th goal in the Premier League against Fulham on the 15th December 2001?

a) Tim Sherwood b) Les Ferdinand c) Teddy Sheringham

41. Who was the oldest first team player for Spurs?

a) Brad Friedel b) Ray Clemence c) Carlo Cudicini

42. There is only one Tottenham player who played for Honduras. Who was he?

a) Giovanni dos Santos b) Federico Fazio c) Wilson Palacios

43. What is Spurs mascot called?

a) Gorgonzola b) Chirpy c) Lilywhite

44. How many league goals did Gus Poyet score for Tottenham?

a) 6 b) 12 c) 18

45. Spurs record away win was against Hull on the 21st May 2017. What was the score?

a) 6 – 1 b) 7 – 1 c) 8 – 1

46. What nationality was Tottenham's first non UK manager?

a) Swedish b) Argentinian c) Swiss

47. Which goalkeeper has played the most games for Spurs?

a) Hugo Lloris b) Ian Walker c) Ted Ditchburn

48. On the 2nd July 2019 Spurs bought Tanguy Ndombele for over £55m from which club?

a) Lyon b) Monaco c) Amiens

49. Who are Spurs' kit suppliers?

a) Nike b) Adidas c) Puma

50. In 1960 – 61 Spurs did the double of League and FA Cup winners. There were 17 players who played in that season. How many of the greatest Spurs team can you name?

Who Said This?

1. Back then, unless you took a machete out on the pitch, you couldn't get booked.
2. I'm very pleased for Paul but it's like watching your mother-in-law drive off a cliff in your new car.
3. If there is a foul you have to fall. I call it 'helping the referee make a decision'.
4. Darren Anderton's had so many x-rays he's got radiation sickness.
5. I'm 58 and I think even I've played more football than Anderton over the past two years.
6. When you finish playing football young man, which is going to be very soon, I feel you will make a very good security guard.
7. He's had a lovely career for the talent he's got.
8. I have just watched the replay, and there is absolutely no doubt: it's inconclusive
9. As we went out on the pitch, he handed me a piece of paper. It was the evening menu for the Liverpool Royal Infirmary.
10. It's easier on the bench, I scored all those we missed today, and three for Southampton.
11. I once said Gazza's IQ is less than his shirt number and he asked me 'What is an IQ?'.
12. I have nothing, nothing to say. Nothing, nothing to say. Nothing to say, I have nothing to say. Nothing to say, I am so sorry, I have nothing to say.

13. I never make predictions and never will.
14. Before Gascoigne, did anyone ever become a national hero and a dead-cert millionaire by crying? Fabulous. Weep and the world weeps with you.
15. We have top players, and sorry if I'm arrogant, we have a top manager.
16. He was a player that hasn't had to use his legs even when he was nineteen years of age because his first two yards were in his head.
17. All the sheep in the country and there is no bacon.
18. Football's football; if it weren't the case it wouldn't be the game it is.
19. I wish Glenn luck but he is putting his head in the frying pan.
20. The biggest thrill of my life was being at my son's birth. I was there because I was suspended.
21. We signed to play until the day we died, and we did.
22. I don't have any tattoos, but that's mainly because none of my limbs are wide enough to support a visible image.
23. Everything in our favour was against us.
24. My wife doesn't like football. One day she called me 10 minutes before a game to find out where I was.
25. If you can't outplay the opposition you must outnumber them.
26. If you want you can make silence very noisy.
27. There was nothing wrong with the performance other than throwing away the game.
28. A game is not won until it is lost.
29. The nice aspect about football is that, if things go wrong, it's the manager who gets the blame.
30. I didn't say them things that I said.

31. Ossie came in the dressing room after the game and handed us £20 or £30 each. He just said, 'Have a good time'. So we all went to the pub.
32. The transfer markets so dead I've been phoning myself and disguising my voice for a bit of interest.
33. I would rather play with 10 men than wait for a player who is late for the bus.
34. Nobody is going to press gang me into anything.
35. I read in the papers that Terry Neil says he's going to put back the joy in Spurs' football. What's he going to do – give them bloody banjos?
36. There used to be a football club over there.
37. I never heard a minute's silence like that.
38. The day I got married, Teddy Sheringham asked for a transfer. I spent my honeymoon in a hotel room with a fax machine trying to sign a replacement.
39. The man we want has to fit a certain profile. Is he a top coach? Would the players respect him? Is he a nutcase?
40. When I go to the press conference before the game, in my mind the game has already started.
41. All I know is that the years '74 to '78 were lost to me.
42. I've been in and out of fashion…mainly out actually.
43. Maybe I can ask the first question. Are there any good diving schools in London?
44. I don't read books. I read the Daily Express and The Star.
45. I write like a two year old and can't spell.
46. I didn't really see my career in football after I'd retired. If I'd known you could get millions for being absolutely crap and getting the sack, I'd have been in like a shot.

47. No boss. I was just going into the club for a nightcap.
48. I prefer players not to be too good or clever at other things.
49. Bill eventually became Mr Tottenham Hotspur and produced such a dazzling team at White Hart Lane that they won the double and played the game in a way that was an object lesson to everybody.
50. The biggest regret of my whole football career was leaving White Hart Lane in 1970. I was heartbroken.

Answers

Quiz 1: The Start Answers

1. It was formed on the 5th September 1882
2. Hotspur Football Club
3. They are the only non-league team to win the FA Cup
4. In 1908 they were elected to the Second Division of the Football League
5. It was Frank Brettell who became manager on the 14th March 1898
6. Portsmouth offered more money
7. They finished second to Bolton Wanderers
8. They beat Wolves 1 - 0.
9. It was 40 years later in 1961
10. It was Billy Minter who scored 95 league goals for Spurs

Quiz 2: Bill Nicholson Answers

1. He was born in Scarborough in 1919
2. Northfleet FC
3. He joined the Durham Light Infantry
4. He played 314 times with his career interrupted by WW2
5. He won 3 – 2nd Division Champions 1949 – 50, 1st Division

Champions1950 – 51 and Charity Shield in 1951

6. He was appointed the manager of Spurs on the 11th October 1958
7. He made one appearance for England against Portugal and scored after 19 seconds
8. Remarkably the score was 10 - 4
9. He was an adviser at West Ham
10. He won the 11 trophies – First Division (1960 – 61), FA Cup (1960 – 61, 1961 – 62 and 1966 – 67), League Cup (1970 – 71 and 1972 – 73), Charity Shield (1961, 1962 and 1967), Uefa Cup (1971 – 72) and the European Cup Winners Cup (1962 – 63)

Quiz 3: Jimmy Greaves Answers

1. Peter
2. He began his professional career in 1957 at Chelsea
3. He made his debut on the 24th August 1957 in a 1 – 1 draw against Tottenham and scored
4. AC Milan
5. He was signed for £99,999. The reason for this was allegedly to relieve Greaves of the pressure of being the first £100,000 footballer
6. He scored 220 goals
7. Martin Peters
8. He scored 44 goals
9. Geoff Hurst
10. It was Ian St John and the program was called Saint and Greavsie

Quiz 4: Jose Mourinho Answers

1. He was born in Portugal
2. Bobby Robson
3. He was appointed Benfica manager in September 2000
4. Van Gaal
5. He won three – EFL Cup 2016 – 17, FA Community Shield 2016 and the UEFA Europa League 2016 – 17
6. He has won the Champions League with Porto in 2003 – 04 and Inter Milan in 2009 – 10
7. They were 14th
8. They finished 6th
9. It was the ball boy for getting the ball back quickly for Spurs to score
10. He called him a voyeur

Quiz 5: Harry Redknapp Answers

1. He is Henry James Redknapp
2. Tottenham
3. It was Juande Ramos
4. They were 20th, and bottom, with only 2 points from 8 games
5. Spurs finished 8th
6. He was appointed Jordan manager in 2016 for 2 matches
7. Frank Lampard Jr is the son of his wife's late sister Patricia
8. He has written, or had ghost written, 4 autobiographies
9. He didn't win any though Spurs were runners up in the League Cup in 2008 – 09
10. I'm a Celebrity. He won it and was named 'King of the Jungle'

Quiz 6: Glenn Hoddle Answers

1. He was born on the 27th October 1957
2. Martin Chivers
3. It was Bill Nicholson
4. Cyril Knowles
5. He played 490 games and scored 110 goals
6. He played 53 games for England
7. He joined AS Monaco
8. George Graham
9. It happened on the 27th October 2018 and it was Hoddle's 61st birthday
10. Chris Waddle

Quiz 7: Steve Perryman Answers

1. He is Stephen John Perryman
2. It was Graeme Souness prior to his move to Middlesbrough
3. He was at Spurs from 1969 to 1986 for a total of 17 years
4. He made a total of 854 appearances for Tottenham
5. He won the award in 1982
6. He won 8 trophies – FA Cup in 1980 – 81 & 1981 – 82, League Cup in 1970 -71 & 1972 – 73, UEFA Cup 1971 – 72 & 1983 – 84, Charity Shield 1981 and the Anglo-Italian League Cup in 1971
7. Oxford United
8. He played 1 game for England against Iceland in 1982 as a 70th minute substitute
9. It was Ossie Ardiles

10. He was player manager at Brentford

Quiz 8: Paul Gascoigne Answers

1. He was born in Gateshead
2. Jack Charlton
3. The contract was for £120/week
4. He had agreed to join Man Utd
5. He spent £70,000 on a house for his parents
6. It was 1990.
7. It was Gary Charles that he fouled while he was playing for Notts Forest
8. He was sold to Lazio
9. He only played 92 league games and scored 19 goals in them
10. It was 'Fog on the Tyne' in collaboration with Lindisfarne

Quiz 9: Mauricio Pochettino Answers

1. He was born in Murphy, Argentina
2. It was Marcelo Bielsa. Newell's Old Boys named their stadium after Bielsa
3. Espanyol
4. He replaced Tim Sherwood
5. Spurs lost 2 – 0 to Chelsea
6. It was against Ajax. Spurs came back from 3 – 0 down with a second half hat trick by Lucas Moura to win on away goals
7. He was in charge for 293 games
8. It was the most yellow cards in a game – 9 in total
9. Chelsea

10. He didn't win any but was the runner up in the 2014 – 15 League Cup, the 2016 – 17 Premier League and the 2018 – 19 Champions League

Quiz 10: Terry Venables Answers

1. He is Terence Frederick Venables
2. It was Chelsea
3. It was Tommy Docherty the Chelsea manager
4. He made 141 appearances and scored 9 goals
5. He played 2 games in 1964.
6. He became Crystal Palace manager in June 1976
7. It was Barcelona
8. He took over from Graham Taylor
9. In November 1996 he was appointed the manager of Australia
10. It was Hazel which was a novel he co-authored and turned into a TV series. There were 22 hour long episodes

Quiz 11: Harry Kane Answers

1. He is Harry Edward Kane
2. He was at Arsenal but was released for being a bit 'chubby and not 'very athletic'.
3. It was Crystal Palace he never featured for
4. It was Sunderland and Spurs won 5 -1 with Kane scoring his first Premier League goal in the 59th minute.
5. It was the Republic of Ireland through his father's side of the family. His father is fluent in Irish Gaelic.
6. It was Gary Lineker in the 1991 – 92 season when he got 28 goals

7. David Beckham attended the same school though several years prior
8. 2014/15
9. It was Jimmy Greaves who took 113 games. Bobby Smith took 134 games and George Hunt in 138 games
10. He has named the dog after Tom Brady the NFL quarter back. Kane is a fan of NFL.

Quiz 12: Gary Mabbutt Answers

1. He was born on the 23rd August 1961
2. He played for Bristol Rovers from 1979 – 82
3. Jack Burkinshaw
4. It was Coventry as he scored the winning own goal in the FA Cup Final in the 1987 final
5. He suffers from Type 1 Diabetes and once appeared on Blue Peter to talk about the condition
6. It was John Fashanu
7. He made 611 appearances, second only to Steve Perryman
8. He scored 38 goals at Spurs
9. It was West Ham and Bobby Moore was his favourite player
10. He won 3 – UEFA Cup 1983, FA Cup 1990 – 91 and the Charity Shield 1991

Quiz 13: Pat Jennings Answers

1. He was born in Newry, Northern Ireland
2. He was signed from Watford
3. 596 games
4. His downfield punt beat Alex Stepney of Man Utd

5. It was Peter Shilton in 1977 – 78 playing for Notts Forest
6. He was sold to Arsenal
7. It was Keith Burkinshaw
8. He played 1,095 games – 52 for Watford, 596 for Spurs, 327 for Arsenal, 119 for Northern Ireland and 1 for Northern Ireland under 23s
9. Ossie Ardiles
10. He achieved it twice. Once with Spurs in 1966 – 67 and once with Arsenal in 1978 - 79

Quiz 14: 1960's Transfers Answers

1. Alan Mullery came from Fulham
2. He arrived from Blackburn
3. Dave McKay
4. Martin Chivers
5. He was signed from Dundee
6. Middlesbrough
7. It was Terry Venables
8. Bobby Smith
9. Southampton
10. It was Arsenal

Quiz 15: 1970's Transfers Answers

1. Martin Peters
2. Burnley
3. It was Alan Mullery who was sent off in a 1968 game against Yugoslavia.

4. It was Norwich
5. Terry Yorath
6. Keith Burkinshaw
7. He was an Argentinian and in the 1978 World Cup winning squad with Ossie Ardiles
8. Peter Taylor who was the England caretaker in 2000 after the departure of Kevin Keegan
9. It was Gerry Armstrong
10. Servette which is a Swiss football club

Quiz 16: 1980's Transfers Answers

1. It was Aberdeen
2. Garth Crooks
3. It was Ray Clemence who went on to play over 300 games for Spurs
4. He joined Blackburn
5. Barcelona
6. He was sold to Marseille
7. They paid £2.2m
8. Paul Allen
9. It was Steve Hodge
10. He was born in Stavanger, Norway

Quiz 17: 1990's Transfers Answers

1. Notts Forest
2. Darren Anderton
3. Liverpool

4. He played two games for Montserrat
5. It was Gerry Francis
6. Middlesbrough
7. £2.5m
8. It was Les Ferdinand
9. Surprisingly he played for Wales. As a British citizen born outside the country he was allowed by the rules at the time to play for any UK country. He chose Wales despite having no family connections.
10. Southampton

Quiz 18: 2000's Transfers Answers

1. He was born in Montevideo and is Uruguayan. He played 26 games for the national team
2. Robbie Keane
3. Aaron Lennon
4. Glenn Hoddle
5. Notts Forest
6. £16.5m
7. It was Darren Bent who also cost £16.5m
8. Portsmouth
9. He was signed from Sheffield United
10. Southampton

Quiz 19: 2010+ Transfers Answers

1. It was Leeds following their relegation to Division 1
2. Togo

3. They offered £15m
4. A bit of a trick question as he was sold by Atletico Madrid but had been on loan to Southampton.
5. They played together at Ajax
6. They paid £85.1m
7. He came from Roma
8. MK Dons
9. He was signed from Portuguese club Sporting CP. His parents had moved to Portugal
10. Bayer Leverkusen

Quiz 20: White Hart Lane Answers

1. They moved there in 1899
2. It was a nursery ground and owned by Charrington Breweries
3. The gate totalled £115
4. Following a share issue to raise funds they paid £8,950 for the ground
5. There were 75,038
6. It was Man Utd and Spurs won 3 – 1. Demolition began the next day
7. The capacity was 36,300
8. The score was 13 – 2
9. The projected cost at the outset was £400m. This rose to £750m by 2017 and the eventual cost is estimated at £1 billion
10. It was Son Heung-min in a 2 – 0 win over Crystal Palace on the 3rd April 2019

Quiz 21: Captains Answers

1. Hugo Lloris
2. Younes Kaboul
3. Michael Dawson
4. Ledley King
5. Jaimie Redknapp
6. Teddy Sheringham
7. Sol Campbell
8. Gary Mabbutt
9. Allan Mullery
10. Danny Blanchflower

Quiz 22: Player of the Year Answers

1. Heung-Min Son
2. Christian Eriksen
3. Toby Alderweireld
4. Scott Parker
5. Luka Modric
6. Jonathan Woodgate
7. Robbie Keane
8. Sol Campbell
9. Jurgen Klinsmann
10. Gary Lineker

Quiz 23: Managers Answers

1. Tim Sherwood
2. Harry Redknapp
3. He is Dutch
4. Jacques Santini
5. Glenn Hoddle
6. He is Swiss
7. Gerry Francis
8. Keith Burkinshaw
9. He was born in Neath, Wales
10. Terry Neil

Quiz 24: First Division 1950 – 51 Champions Answers

1. This was the first time Spurs won the title, so 0 is the answer
2. It was Man Utd who were 4 points behind
3. Alf Ramsey
4. Sonny Walters with 15 goals
5. Arthur Rowe
6. It was the push and run which was like a wall pass
7. It was Ron Burgess
8. Bill Nicholson
9. They were the first team to win the First and Second Division in successive seasons
10. They finished second to Man Utd

Quiz 25: First Division 1960 – 61 Champions Answers

1. It had been done twice before in 1889 – 90 by Preston and 1896 – 97 by Aston Villa
2. Sheffield Wednesday
3. Bill Nicholson
4. It was Bobby Smith who scored 32 goals this season, including 5 in the FA Cup
5. It was Danny Blanchflower
6. It was Bill Brown though John Hollowbread did play 1 league game
7. They scored 115 goals. Second placed Sheffield Weds scored 78 goals.
8. It was Les Allen whose son Clive played for Spurs
9. There were 3 Scottish players for Spurs in 1960 – 61 – Dave MacKay, Bill Brown and John White
10. They finished 3rd. Alf Ramsey's Ipswich Town won the league

Quiz 26: FA Cup 1960 – 61 Winner Answers

1. Wolves
2. They had won it twice in 1900 – 01 and 1920 – 21
3. It was Leicester
4. Spurs won 2 – 0
5. Frank McClintock
6. Gordon Banks
7. They beat Burnley 3 – 0
8. The Leicester v Sheff Utd semi-final went to a second replay after two 0 – 0 draws. The first goal was in the 47th minute of the second replay

9. It was Terry Dyson
10. Bobby Smith scored 5 goals, Les Allen scored 4 goals and Cliff Jones scored 4 goals as well

Quiz 27: UEFA Cup 1971 – 72 Winner Answers

1. It was the Inter Cities Fairs Cup
2. Spurs won 15 – 1 on aggregate. It was 6 – 1 away and 9 – 0 at White Hart Lane
3. Iceland
4. It was Wolverhampton Wanderers.
5. Allan Mullery
6. It was Joe Kinnear who played 26 times for the Republic of Ireland. Derek Dougan played for Northern Ireland
7. Martin Chivers scored the most goals with 8. Gilzean got 6 and Mullery 4. In total 11 different players scored for Spurs during the competition
8. AC Milan
9. It was Liverpool
10. Bill Nicholson

Quiz 28: FA Cup 1990 – 91 Winner Answers

1. It was Terry Venables
2. Notts Forest
3. Garry Mabbutt
4. It was Des Walker who scored an own goal in extra time
5. They have won the FA Cup 8 times
6. It was Dave Beasant who in the 1988 final saved a Liverpool penalty, taken by John Aldridge, to ensure victory for

Wimbledon

7. It was Nayim
8. Erik Thorsvedt
9. They beat Arsenal 3 – 1
10. It was Paul Gascoigne who scored 6 goals

Quiz 29: 1983 – 84 UEFA Cup Winner Answers

1. It was Anderlecht
2. Hajduk Split
3. It emerged during a 1997 criminal case that Anderlecht admitted paying the referee £27,000 to make sure Anderlecht won. Needless to say, Anderlecht won after a number of controversial refereeing decisions
4. The final was a two legged affair and Spurs won 4 – 3 on penalties after the second leg
5. Steve Perryman
6. They lost 1 – 0 to Real Madrid
7. It was Tony Parkes
8. Steve Archibald
9. It was Keith Burkinshaw and his last game in charge. He left shortly after winning the cup due to a disagreement with the board
10. It was Frank Arnesen

Quiz 30: 1966 – 67 FA Cup Winner Answers

1. It was Chelsea
2. Spurs won 2 – 1
3. It was Everton who beat Sheffield Wednesday in the 1966

final 3 – 2

4. It was the first all London final
5. They beat Notts Forest 2 – 1
6. Dave McKay
7. It was Peter Bonetti, who was back up for Gordon Banks, but never played in the 1966 World Cup
8. It was Frank Saul and Jimmy Robertson
9. It was Pat Jennings
10. There were three – Dave McKay, Frank Saul and Cliff Jones

Quiz 31: 2007 –08 League Cup Winner Answers

1. It was known as the Carling Cup
2. They beat Chelsea 2 – 1 after extra time
3. Johnathan Woodgate
4. Arsenal
5. It was Juande Ramos
6. Didier Zakora
7. Pau Robinson
8. It was Ledley King
9. Wayne Bridge
10. He comes from Finland

Quiz 32: Son Heung-Min Answers

1. He was born on the 8th July 1992
2. He joined Hamburg in August 2008
3. According to his agent it was from watching SpongeBob in German

4. He came from Bayer Leverkusen
5. £22m
6. He was part of the team that won the Asian games which was one of the ways to get exemption from National Service
7. It was Southampton who they beat 5 – 2
8. It was 2019 – 20 with a goal he scored against Burnley on the 7th December 2019
9. It was in a 3 – 0 victory over Leeds
10. He has a sponsorship deal with Adidas

Quiz 33: Danny Blanchflower Answers

1. He was born in Belfast, Northern Ireland
2. He joined the RAF as a trainee navigator
3. Barnsley
4. Spurs paid Aston Villa £30,000
5. He played 382 games for Spurs and scored on 21 occasions
6. He became the manager of Chelsea
7. Apartheid
8. He famously refused to appear on This is Your Life hosted by Eamon Andrews. He viewed it as an invasion of privacy
9. It was his younger brother Jackie Blanchflower
10. He won 4 – First Division 1960 – 61, FA Cup 1960 – 61 and 1961 – 62 and the European Cup Winners Cup in 1962 - 63

Quiz 34: Ledley King Answers

1. Brenton
2. George Graham in May 1999 in a 3 – 2 defeat at Anfield

3. It was scored in 9.82 seconds which was the fastest Premier League goal at the time
4. He played 323 games in a career blighted by knee injuries
5. On the 6th August 2020 King was appointed Assistant Coach to Mourinho
6. He was never Player of the Year
7. King captained Spurs for 7 seasons before he retired in 2012
8. It was erected in Mile End Park
9. His shirt number was 26
10. He won just one trophy, the League Cup in 2008 when they beat Chelsea 2 - 1

Quiz 35: Cyril Knowles Answers

1. Barry
2. He played Rugby League
3. Middlesbrough
4. Bill Nicholson paid £45,000 for him
5. It was sung by The Cockerel Chorus it reached number 14 and gained an Ivor Novello Award for the Best Novel Song of 1974
6. He played left back
7. He played 506 games for Spurs scoring 17 goals
8. He got 4 England caps
9. He won 6 trophies – FA Cup 1967, Charity Shield 1967, League Cup in 1970 – 71 and 1972 – 73, Anglo Italian 1971 and UEFA Cup 1971 – 72
10. He became a Jehovah's Witness

Quiz 36: Hugo Lloris Answers

1. How's your geography, it is on the south coast of France on the Mediterranean Sea
2. He was born on 26th December 1986
3. Tennis
4. Lyon
5. It was Brad Friedel who made way
6. The lost in the quarter-finals to Germany 1 - 0
7. They beat Belgium 1 – 0
8. It was Thibaut Courtois
9. He was captain for the 2015 – 16 season
10. It was 2016 – 17 when they finished second to Chelsea

Quiz 37: Chris Hughton Answers

1. He was born on the 11th December 1958
2. He trained as a lift engineer
3. He played left back
4. Keith Burkinshaw
5. He played 398 games scoring 19 times
6. He played for the Republic of Ireland despite being born in Forest Gate, Essex
7. West Ham
8. He won 4 trophies – the FA Cup 1980 – 81 and 1981 – 82, UEFA Cup 1983 – 84 and the Charity Shield in 1981
9. It was 12 managers – Keith Burkinshaw, Peter Shreeves, Ray Clemence, Doug Livermore, Osvaldo Ardiles, Gerry Francis, Christian Gross, George Graham, Glenn Hoddle, David Pleat,

Jacques Santini and Martin Jol

10. He was appointed Newcastle manager in 2009

Quiz 38: Jermain Defoe Answers

1. He is Jermain Colin Defoe
2. A trick question because surprisingly they all played for Senrab
3. His debut was for West Ham in September 2000 in a League Cup game against Walsall
4. He scored a total of 143 goals
5. He was the leading scorer in two seasons – 2004 – 05 (22 goals) and 2009 – 10 (24 goals)
6. Portsmouth
7. £15.75m
8. It supports young people and resulted in Defoe getting an OBE in the 2018 Birthday Honours
9. It was on the 25th October 2020 for Rangers against Livingston
10. He played 57 times for England scoring 20 goals

Quiz 39: Jan Vertonghen

1. He was born in Belgium on the 24th April 1987
2. Ajax
3. He cost €12 million
4. Andre Villas-Boas had been manager for 5 days when Vertonghen was signed
5. It was Marouane Fellaini
6. He played 315 games for Spurs

7. He joined Benfica
8. 2018
9. It was in the Champions League semi final against Ajax in April 2019.
10. It was Martin Jol

Quiz 40: Martin Chivers Answers

1. He is Martin Harcourt Chivers
2. It was Southampton
3. Nicholson paid £125,000, a club record at the time, with Frank Saul going the other way
4. He read on a billboard outside The Echo offices 'Chivers to Spurs'
5. He was the leading scorer in 5 seasons – 1969 – 70 (11 goals), 1970 – 71 (34 goals), 1971 – 72 (44 goals), 1972 – 73 (33 goals) and 1973 – 74 (23 goals)
6. He played 367 games
7. Jermain Defoe scored 23 European goals for Spurs
8. Servette is in Switzerland
9. He played 24 games for England scoring 13 goals
10. The title was 'Big Chiv: My Goals in Life'. 'Anything is possible' is Gareth Southgate's and 'I'll Tell You What…' is Robbie Savage's

Quiz 41: Alan Gilzean Answer's

1. He was born on the 22nd October 1938
2. Dundee
3. He scored 169 league goals for Dundee

4. He cost £72,500
5. He played 439 times for Spurs scoring 133 goals
6. He was never the leading goal scorer. Despite his 133 goals his main role was provider for firstly Jimmy Greaves then Martin Chivers
7. He played 22 times for Scotland scoring 12 goals
8. He had a desk job at a transport company
9. He won 5 trophies – UEFA Cup 1972, FA Cup 1967, the Charity Shield 1967 and the League Cup in 1971 and 1973
10. He was the King of White Hart Lane

Quiz 42: Robbie Keane Answers

1. He was born in Dublin on 8th July 1980
2. Wolverhampton Wanderers
3. He only played 6 games. Lippi, who signed him was promptly sacked, and Keane was deemed surplus
4. David O'Leary
5. It is Shay Given who received 134 caps
6. He was number 10
7. It was Edgar Davids but all was resolved later
8. He played 125 league games for LA Galaxy scoring 83 goals
9. It was Teddy Sheringham
10. He was Player of the Year 3 times – 2003, 2005 – 06 and 2007 – 08

Quiz 43: Christian Eriksen Answers

1. He was born on the 14th February 1992
2. He arrived from Ajax with a reported transfer fee of £11m

3. It was Erik Lamela who joined from Roma
4. Andre Villas-Boas
5. Inter Milan
6. Alexis Sanchez
7. He played 305 games scoring 69 goals
8. 23
9. She is Louise Dannemann Eriksen
10. He was Player of the Year twice in 2013 – 14 and 2016 - 17

Quiz 44: Aaron Lennon Answers

1. He is Aaron Justin Lennon
2. He was 14 and sponsored by Adidas
3. He was 16 years 129 days
4. £1m
5. Martin Jol
6. He played 364 games for Spurs scoring 30 goals
7. £4.5m
8. They are from Turkey
9. He has 21 caps
10. The League Cup in 2007 - 08

Quiz 45: Darren Anderton Answers

1. He was born on the 3rd March 1972
2. Portsmouth
3. He cost Spurs £1.75m
4. He was called Sicknote due to the number of injuries he sustained

5. He played 384 games for Spurs scoring 48 goals
6. He left for Birmingham
7. Jacques Santini
8. Bournemouth in the 2008 – 09 season
9. 1993
10. He played 30 times scoring 7 goals

Quiz 46: Bobby Smith Answers

1. He was born on 22nd February 1933
2. It was Chelsea
3. £18,000
4. It was £17/week. He was 28 before he earned over £20/week.
5. He scored 208 goals
6. It was Brighton
7. He became a painter and decorator
8. Chelsea apparently send £1500 to surviving members of the Championship winning squad
9. He played 15 times and scored 13 goals
10. The medal sold for £11,200

Quiz 47: Michael Dawson Answers

1. He is Michael Richard Dawson
2. He turned professional in 2000 with Notts Forest
3. Andy Reid
4. He played 324 games for Spurs
5. He scored 10 goals
6. He was captain for 4 seasons – 2009 – 10, 2010 – 11, 2011 –

12 and 2012 – 13

7. He went to Hull for a fee of around £3.5m
8. He played 4 games for England
9. 2009 -10
10. It was Robbie Keane who left on loan to Celtic

Quiz 48: Jurgen Klinsmann Answers

1. He served an apprenticeship as a baker. His family operate a bakery in Stuttgart
2. Germany beat Argentina 1 – 0 in the final
3. Monaco
4. £2 million
5. They finished 7th
6. He was manager of the USA from July 2011 to November 2016
7. He played 68 games for Spurs
8. He scored 38 goals
9. West Germany won the bronze medal
10. It was against Wimbledon

Quiz 49: Osvaldo Ardiles Answers

1. He is Argentinian
2. Keith Burkinshaw
3. It was Ricardo Villa
4. Chas & Dave. The song reached number 5
5. The Falklands War against Argentina.
6. Blackburn

7. He was appointed manager of Swindon
8. 10 days after promotion was gained by Swindon it was taken away due to irregular payments to players
9. It was Gerry Francis
10. The Falkland Islands

Quiz 50: Miscellaneous Answers

1. It is Bobby Smith
2. Ronnie Rosenthal
3. He played for Nagoya Grampus in Japan
4. It was scored from the halfway line
5. A trick question as all three are correct. Spurs are the only non league club to win the FA Cup. A crowd of 110, 820 in Crystal palace was a world record and Sandy Brown was the first player to score in every round.
6. It was Diego Maradona
7. It was Clive Allen who in the 1986 – 87 season scored 33 league goals and 49 in all competitions
8. Harry Hotspur was the nickname given to Sir Henry Percy (1364 – 1403) who saw action in the Hundred Years War
9. It is Audere Est Facere (to dare is to do). The others are the Apollo mission and the SAS
10. He is Argentinian
11. It was Holsten in 1983
12. AIA have an 8 year deal costing £40-45m per year
13. It is an insurance company
14. It was in 1983 and was delisted in 2012
15. It was 85,512 against Bayer Leverkusen on the 2nd November

2016 at Wembley

16. Crewe Alexandra
17. In 1976 – 77 finished last in the old First Division but were promoted back the following season
18. They paid Barcelona £1.1m for Lineker
19. He scored 67 league goals in 105 games for Tottenham
20. He was killed by lightening while sheltering under a tree while playing golf. He left a 21 year old widow and three children
21. He was signed from Southampton
22. He is Brazilian
23. It was Gareth Bale
24. He was born in Bulgaria
25. It was against Watford who had Ben Foster in goal
26. Newcastle
27. It was Gordon Durie who scored in their third game of the campaign in a 2 – 2 draw with Crystal Palace
28. It is 86.8m long
29. Dier moved to live in Portugal when he was 7 and grew up there and was approached to play for their national team prior to committing to England
30. It was in 2016 – 17 when they finished 2nd to Chelsea
31. The first game was against Crystal Palace and Spurs won 2 – 0
32. They sell online cars
33. They have won the FA Cup 8 times – 1900 – 01, 1920 – 21, 1960 – 61, 1961 – 62, 1966 – 67, 1980 – 81, 1981 – 82 and 1990 – 91
34. Erik Thorsvedt

35. On the 10th January 2021 Alfie Devine scored against Marine aged 16 years 163 days

36. Eric Dier

37. It was 37 years since the previous sending off for Spurs which happened on the 27th October 1928 against Stoke

38. They had nine players booked, but no sendings off

39. Unlike Pochettino who was sent off 13 times in his career

40. Les Ferdinand

41. It was Brad Friedel on March 20th, 2014 against Benfica in the Europa League. He was 42 years 10 months and 2 days

42. Wilson Palacios

43. Chirpy

44. He scored 18 goals

45. The score at Hull was 7 – 1

46. It was Ossie Ardiles who is Argentinian

47. It was Ted Ditchburn who played 452 games for Spurs between 1946 and 1958

48. It was Lyon

49. Nike

50. Bill Brown (48 games), Peter Baker (48 games), Ron Henry (49 games), Danny Blanchflower (49 games), Maurice Norman (48 games), Dave MacKay (44 games), Cliff Jones (34 games), John White (49 games), Bobby Smith (43 games), Les Allen (49 games), Terry Dyson (47 games), Terry Medwin (16 games), Frank Saul (6 games), Tony Marchi (6 games), John Hollowbread (1 game), Ken Barton (1 game) and John Smith (1 game)

Who Said This? Answers

1. Jimmy Greaves
2. Terry Venables on the sale of Paul Gascoigne
3. Jose Mourinho
4. Sir Alan Sugar
5. Jimmy Greaves
6. David Pleat to Razor Ruddock
7. David Pleat talking about Peter Crouch
8. Garth Crooks
9. Jimmy Greaves on Tommy Smith
10. Jimmy Greaves after being rested for a game before an important cup semi-final
11. George Best
12. Jose Mourinho
13. Paul Gascoigne
14. Salman Rushdie
15. Jose Mourinho
16. Glenn Hoddle
17. Paul Gascoigne at a New Zealand hotel
18. Garth Crooks

19. Ossie Ardiles on Glenn Hoddle and the England job
20. Razor Ruddock
21. Jimmy Greaves
22. Peter Crouch
23. Danny Blanchflower
24. Peter Crouch
25. Terry Venables
26. Jose Mourinho
27. Glenn Hoddle
28. David Pleat
29. Gary Lineker
30. Glenn Hoddle
31. Jurgen Klinsmann
32. Gerry Francis
33. Jose Mourinho
34. Danny Blanchflower on turning down 'This is Your Life'
35. Eddie Bailey
36. Keith Burkinshaw
37. Glenn Hoddle
38. Gerry Francis
39. David Pleat
40. Jose Mourinho
41. Jimmy Greaves
42. Peter Crouch
43. Jurgen Klinsmann at his first Spurs press conference

44. Tim Sherwood
45. Harry Redknapp during his fracas with the taxman
46. Jimmy Greaves on taking up management
47. Alan Gilzean to Bill Nicholson after being spotted by a fan leaving a nightclub at 2am
48. Bill Nicholson
49. Brian Clough
50. Jimmy Greaves

ONE LAST THING...

If you have enjoyed this book I would love you to write a review of the book on Amazon. It is really useful feedback as well as giving untold encouragement to the author.

If you have any comments, corrections, suggestions for improvements or for other books I would love to hear from you, and you can contact me at; m.prefontaine2@gmail.com

Your comments are greatly valued, and the books have been revised and improved as a result of helpful suggestions from readers

Printed in Great Britain
by Amazon

69422326R00071